Adventures of a
Tibetan Fighting Monk

A SIAN
PORTRAITS

VISAGES
D'ASIE

ADVENTURES OF A
TIBETAN FIGHTING MONK

Tashi Khedrup

Compiled by
Hugh Richardson

Edited by
Tadeusz Skorupski

Orchid Press
Bangkok 1998

Tashi Khedrup
ADVENTURES OF A TIBETAN FIGHTING MONK
Compiled by Hugh Richardson *Edited by* Tadeusz Skorupski

First Published 1986
Reprinted 1998

Orchid Press
98/13 Soi Apha Phirom, Ratchada Road,
Chatuchak, Bangkok 10900, Thailand

ISBN 974-8299-17-1

Contents

Foreword

In 1959 the Rockefeller Foundation saw, with praiseworthy rapidity, that the stream of refugees reaching India and Nepal after the unsuccessful rising against the Chinese occupation of Tibet had brought within the reach of western scholars an unprecedented wealth of native Tibetan learning and experience. As a result of a conference at the Villa Serbelloni on Lake Como, under the chairmanship of Mr. Chadbourne Gilpatric, the Foundation gave grants enabling representative Tibetan scholars or Tibetans possessing some special experience to be invited to the principal centres of Tibetan studies in six European countries, the U.S.A. and Japan.

The School of Oriental and African Studies at the University of London was one of those centres. Dr. D.L. Snellgrove, then Reader in Tibetan there, and already well acquainted with India and Nepal, visited those countries in search of suitable persons and eventually returned with five Tibetans. Tashi Khedrup, the teller of this story, was one. The impetus given to Tibetan studies by that development has been considerable. It has contributed to the publication of valuable works, including those by Dr. Snellgrove, in a field hardly touched by western scholars — The *Nine Ways of Bon*, and *Four Lamas of Dolpo*.

When the Rockefeller Foundation's grant came to an end in 1965, the usefulness of the visiting Tibetans was far from exhausted. Lack of money to continue the programme led to a reduction of the number of Tibetans to two, for whom support had to be found in other ways. Rather than allow interest in Tibetan studies to be devitalized by the absence of Tibetan helpers, Dr. Snellgrove, on his own initiative and largely with his own resources, established an Institute of Tibetan Studies with a small residential headquarters at Tring.

Tashi's story is a very small part of that experience, but his progression from Tibetan village boy to British national contains enough of the usual and the unusual to be worth recording. In Tibet, none but important holy men were the subjects of biography, and their stories concentrate on spiritual experience to the exclusion of nearly everything else. Since the great exodus to India, the lead in biography of a different and more general nature has been given by the Dalai Lama himself. This lead has been followed by his brother Tagtsher Rimpoche and a few other important personages. Tashi's story, from a lower place in the social hierarchy, should prove a valuable complement to those of the great.

This book has grown from leisurely talks over the past six years or so, in a mixture of English and Tibetan, sometimes at Tring, sometimes in our house in Scotland. During nine years in Tibet I came to know something of the setting of Tashi's life. I have been in his native village, visited his monastery and his sub — college, been a guest in Lhasa houses which he visited, attended the New Year ceremonies, and camped in the grazing uplands, I was in Lhasa at the time of the Reting troubles, which I saw from a different angle. Although I may have had a fleeting glimpse of Tashi in the refugee camp at Misamari in 1960, so far as we know our paths never crossed in Tibet. I have learned with amused surprise that he, and, I suppose, the majority of his fellow monks, was unaware of the existence of a representative at Lhasa of the British Government. For my part, although there was no difficulty in meeting and talking to ordinary monks, villagers and herdsmen, and in seeing their way of life, conversation with them was — with a very few exceptions — only casual. It was with the noble officials and high lamas, with whom the contacts of our diplomatic mission were inevitably most intimate, that serious discussion was possible. And so Tashi's account of his life has revealed the ways and thinking of a layer of Tibetan society of which I knew little. Listening to him, I was frequently struck by echoes of cha- racteristics I have long admired in his fellow countrymen – self – reliant competence and adaptability without a trace of self – satisfaction or arrogance; sympathetic tolerance and readiness to help others with complete absence of snobbery; a strong moral conscience; gaiety; gentle- ness and good humour. I found reinforcement for my strong impression that the great and simple share essentially the same way of thinking and that the social gap between them is remarkably narrow. The material has, of course, been arranged, but not at the expense of the natural simplicity of Tashi's narrative. He was in no way concerned to point morals. From what I knew of the background I was able to turn his thoughts into channels that interested me. However, I did all I could to avoid putting thoughts into his head, and I have tried to record only what he said and not what I saw for myself. It has been a fascinating and enjoyable task. I hope it may prove good reading.

                                                                Hugh Richardson

I
TSHAPANANG VILLAGE

I was born in the village of Tshapanang, about thirty miles downstream from Lhasa in the valley of the Kyi river. I can't say just when. Tibetan villagers don't pay much attention to dates and so on. It was certainly a Wednesday, for that is the meaning of Lhakpa, the name I was first given. My father and mother could have told me whether it was winter or summer, and could have identified the year by its animal sign; but that didn't seem important to me in Tibet, and it does not seem important even now. Still, to satisfy my friends in Britain I have tried to work it out with their help; and if, as I think, I was born in a rat year it was probably late in 1937.

Tshapanang is quite a big village belonging mostly to the monastery of Sera near Lhasa. My father, Tseten Dorje, was one of the headmen; my mother was from the same village and owned some fields there. She had been a shepherd girl before she married and was very clever with the animals. She didn't lose any sheep; and lots of lambs were born and grew up safely while she was looking after them. It was the custom for work of that sort to be well rewarded, so she was given good clothes and some small fields. These were her own property; she paid no tax to anyone for them and could give them away or sell them, provided it was to someone in the same village. They were not very big, but they did make a useful addition to the family income. Father had no fields of his own, but farmed quite a lot of land as a tenant of the monastery, to which he paid all the usual taxes. He would not have been allowed to leave the land; but he never wanted to, for he had a good house of his own there, and a good livelihood.

Tshapanang was a fertile place and, unlike most villages in that part, it was possible to grow two crops a year. The first one, sown in the winter and harvested about June, was the better. Most of that went to the monastery; but the second, sown immediately after the ground was cleared, and reaped about October, went almost all to us. As a large amount of the manure from Sera monastery was always sent to our village, it was really quite a good crop most years.

In addition, we had some horses, mules, bullocks, cows, *dzo* — which are half – bred yaks for ploughing — donkeys, pigs and hens. All that was our own and we paid only a small tax — two sheep a year, a pig at the New Year, and 600 eggs. And, since Tshapanang was on the main road, we were responsible for a share of the *ula* service. That meant providing animals to carry the baggage of government officials when they were travelling our way. This duty was strictly controlled, and those who had to do it paid rather less tax on their crops.

Father was short and sturdy like me. He had a strong beard, which is unusual in Tibet and is much admired, but often goes with rather less hair on the head. His manner was calm, kind, but determined. The rest of the villagers always turned to him in any question about their duties or their rights because, although he could not read or write, he had an able, practical mind and a good knowledge of custom and tradition. He knew how to stand up for the village and talk convincingly to officials without annoying them. Mother was active and capable, and a very good manager of the house. She set great store by good manners and was strict with us about that, but always in a gentle and affectionate way.

From seeing people in India and Europe I realize that Tibetans are generally restrained and undemonstrative in their behaviour. Most of them nevertheless, have strong characters and minds of their own, and my mother was never afraid to discuss matters with my father openly and on equal terms. Although Tibetans do not make a great display of their feelings, they do feel deeply, but seem to have a natural tolerance which almost always prevents violent scenes and wrangling. Certainly I never saw any hint of anger between my father and mother.

In our family there were two elder brothers and two elder sisters. The oldest brother I never saw. He disappeared from the house before I was born. Perhaps there was some disagreement with our parents or perhaps he just longed for adventure. He was said to have gone to India and he may be there now for all I know. Then came my eldest sister Dekyi Drokar, then another brother, Dorje; and another sister, Yangchen. As the youngest I was, of course, spoilt, especially by my mother and oldest sister. We had a young servant girl in the house who had run away from her master in Phenpo, north of Lhasa. She had been married to a donkey driver but he was killed in a fight. When she was left a widow the other women in the household used to bully her and make her do all the work. If her master had wanted to send after her she would have had to go back, and would probably have been punished; but that sort of thing didn't happen often. There was an old man, too, who looked after our donkeys and pigs, but he didn't live with the family.

Our house, called Dekyi Khangsar — "The New House of Happiness" — stood a little way off the main road, surrounded by poplar and willow trees. A stout wooden door led out of a narrow lane into a large courtyard with open stabling on three sides of it. Here travellers and traders used to keep their animals and baggage for the night. At the north side of the courtyard was the house with its entrance to one side. Like most Tibetan houses it was built round a small central open space. The door from the courtyard led to our own stables where we kept our horses, cattle, ploughs and so on. That took up all the lower part of the building, for Tibetans did not like to live on the ground floor. There was a steep wooden stair from the stable up to the living quarters. These overlooked three sides of the little inner court. A narrow terrace ran round the inner side with rooms opening off it.

First, through a door covered with a heavy homespun curtain, came the kitchen, the most important room in the house. It was long, narrow and rather dark, though it had small windows with wooden frames covered in oiled paper. The earthen cooking – stove stood along the back wall. During the winter there would be a brazier in the middle of the room, with turf and sheep dung smouldering on it, for extra warmth. There was no chimney, and the smoke escaped through a hole in the ceiling. A couple of low divans, stuffed with hair and covered with rough hide with some bits of rather worn carpet on them, stood along the wall; brass and copper cooking – pots shone on the shelves and various useful things hung from pegs — baskets, ropes, the scarlet lumes for our plough cattle, and so on. Bags of *tsampa* — roasted barley meal — and jugs of *chang* — barley beer — stood in one corner, and our bedding was rolled up in another. For this was the centre of the family; we ate and usually slept here too. Opposite the kitchen, on the other side of the little court-yard, was a store room where the main stock of *tsampa*, oil and other supplies was kept, also bridles, harness and odds and ends. There were usually some hens roosting there in baskets, and the maid servant slept there. Beyond was another small room where my father and mother might sleep if it was not being used by visitors.

The best room was reached by a door beyond the kitchen. It took up most of the south side of the house, overlooking the inner courtyards and catching all the sun without too much wind. This was our chapel and reception room. It had large windows covered with white cotton stretched over carved wooden frames. The floor gleamed with a kind of Tibetan concrete, called *arka*, which takes on a splendid reddish colour and a high polish. We kept it in condition with plenty of candle wax, which my father brought from Lhasa and which we rubbed in by sliding over the floor with felt pads on our feet. In this room was the family altar with images of the great teacher Tsong-ka-pa, the gentle Droma, and other deities. A painted banner of the fierce – looking protector, Tamdrin, hung beside it. There were always butter – lamps on the altar, and a rice offering, and rows of little metal bowls with an offering of clear water in them. Incense was kept burning there all the time. We hardly used the room ourselves, except for family ceremonies at the New Year, but sometimes my father invited a party of monks to perform a religious ceremony there for the good of the family. However, if travellers of importance — lamas or officials came, they would be put up in the chapel room. This was then decorated by hanging a small silk canopy over the low cushioned seats which occupied the place of honour. Rugs were spread on the seats and on the floor; and if we hadn't enough we would borrow from the neighbours.

The flat roof was reached by a ladder. At each corner of it was a cluster of sticks with prayer flags fluttering from them, and a big whitewashed pot for incense which someone, usually my mother, would light first thing every morning. The sweet smoke of wormwood or azalea would rise coiling into the air, as it also did from the roofs of all our neighbours. There was also a small square turret in the middle of the roof, just over the altar in the room below, with sockets on either side which could hold poles. From these we flew large prayer flags on special occasions, for example on the New Year and the birthday of the Dalai Lama.

An important room in every house is the privy. In some houses it is in a small turret built out on the north side, with an opening at ground level for clearing the manure out of the pit. Our little turret was on the ground floor, at a corner of the stable. It was kept tidy and inoffensive by shovelling earth into it when necessary; and it was cleared every spring when the manure was put on the fields. That might not do in a climate like England, but in the dry air of Tibet it gave no trouble or nuisance.

What made our house one of the best in the village was its big courtyard. There was space for a large number of animals and their drivers, so traders and travellers found it a good place to stop. The richer travellers usually hired a room in our house; and as they needed fodder for the animals and *chang* for themselves, that brought in a good profit. In addition, we had a row of small ovens along the south wall of the house. Here the villagers would bring their barley to roast for a small fee. So we were quite well off and I don't think my father had any debts. In many places farmers do have long – standing debts to the landlords, because if there is a bad crop one year they have to borrow seed for the next, or even barley to eat, and then they go on paying interest on the loan. Sometimes the steward of an estate would not demand interest in cash or in grain, but if a man had a pony or a cow, it might be treated as security for the debt. If either had a foal or a calf, that would be taken as payment. Certainly it gave a landlord a hold over his farmers if they were always owing him something. Some people got into such difficulties that their debts kept mounting year by year and they could not possibly pay. When the Dalai Lama came of age he had a great many of the old debts cancelled. But Tshapanang was fertile, and crops there were generally good. I can't remember any people in the village who were really poor, and certainly there was never any sign of starvation. No one would have been allowed to get into such a condition in our neighbourhood.

In fact, looking back, it seems to have been a fairly easy life. Although my father was always busy with his duties as headman and his business of hiring animals, there never seemed to be a hurry, and he found time now and then to go with his ponies to Lhasa. As the return journey took three or four days, he usually paid someone from the village to go for him.

One thing Father always did himself was to plough our fields. The season started with a ceremony in the first field. Our plough cattle were beautifully decorated with red tassels, and big collars ornamented with shells and small bells. A Bonpo priest, dressed in white, was in charge of the ceremony and made offerings at a white stone set up in the middle of the field. It was sacred to the spirits of the soil and water, and was always treated with care and respect. After the ceremony the ploughing could start. The women followed behind the plough scattering the seed. But that was just the ceremonial beginning. There would be a break for drinking tea and *chang;* then everyone would get into proper working clothes and the real work began. We were very proud of our plough cattle and Father often gave them special soup in the winter. When they had finished work on our land, he would hire them out to the neighbours.

There were other ceremonies, too, in the fields. In summer a procession went all round the village praying for a good crop. The service was led this time by a monk or a lama, and a good – looking girl and a handsome young man were chosen to take part. They were dressed up in very fine clothes; the girl wearing a headdress of small pearls, and good jewellery of gold and turquoise; the boy in yellow silk. The finery was usually borrowed from some rich neighbour, and even the noblemen of Lhasa were happy to lend valuable things for these occasions. The rest of the villagers followed in their best clothes. Many of them carried great volumes of holy books, in wooden covers, on their backs. Sometimes, if the rain was late in coming, people would go round the village throwing ladles of water on each other to bring the rain. And there was always a good celebration when the harvest was over.

Those things were part of my life. Of course, I don't remember exactly seeing them in my early days, any more than I remember things that happened to me then; but my mother and elder sister used to tell me little things about my childhood. Only one was really dramatic.

Dekyi Drokar used to look after me most of the time so that Mother could get on with the work of the house and the farm. My other sister, Yangchen, used to go out to earn money by working for a neighbour; and it was her job, too, to do all the *ula* tasks which were our family's share. One day in winter Dekyi Drokar had to take some barley to the mill. She loaded the sacks onto a bullock and put me on top. We had to go along a narrow path beside the lade that took water from the river down to the wooden paddles that drove the millstone. Just as we reached the mill, the bullock jumped over the stream and slipped on the other bank so that I fell headlong into the stream. It was covered with ice. I went through and was carried under it by the current towards the mill sluice. Fortunately I stuck on a stump and Dekyi Drokar, who was terribly frightened, managed to break the ice and pull me out. She thought I was drowned, but I revived after a time.

Most Tibetan children get burned sometime or other, playing too near the kitchen stove; and there are marks on my body to show that I was no exception.

The next event was one that decided my way of life. It was harvest time and mother took me to the fields where I was left to play about while she worked. Some chaff must have blown into my right eye and started an inflammation that grew worse and worse even though mother smeared it well with butter. She was worried and decided to take me to consult Sharpa Trulku, an incarnate Lama of Sera who was famous for his skill in healing. She wrapped me in a blanket and carried me all the way to a hermitage on the hillside above Sera monastery, where the Lama was staying at the time. It must have taken her at least two days. The Lama examined my eye and kept us a few days while he treated it. When my eye was better and mother was thinking about taking me home, she went to make an offering to the Lama and get his blessing for us both. He asked her to leave me with him so that I might become a monk, and be one of his personal attendants when I grew up. It would have been difficult for her to refuse. She was very devout, and was pleased that a son of hers should be chosen by an important Lama to become a monk. But my father was not so pleased! He had only one other son at home, and did not get much help from him because he worked as a shepherd for the monastery estates. Father had hoped I would grow up to be useful to him on the farm and with his animals. But there it was. I became a monk — a very little one. In fact I could only just walk. I suppose I was about four years old.

I was given a good wash and my head was shaved. Then I took vows not to have anything to do with women and not to have private property — at least the vows were recited to me and I was told what to answer. I was dressed in the dark red robe of a monk and given a new name, Tendzin Khedrup, to mark my entry into the order. The Lama himself arranged for the necessary offerings that had to be given on my behalf: a white scarf, a silver coin, and a pot of tea. Then my mother had to leave me and go off home alone. I was handed over to the Lama's Assistant Treasurer, who looked after his household and estates. Several Treasurers or Chandzo, as they are called in Tibetan, come into my story. This one was known as Dote Chandzo from the name of the estate to which he was attached.

II
SERA MONASTERY

Sera monastery is a cluster of large white buildings with black –
framed windows, sheltering at the foot of a mountain two miles north
of Lhasa. From the monastery Lhasa can be seen across a sandy plain.
Inside the monastery enclosure are four great assembly halls, with paved
courtyards in front of them. Wide stone steps lead up to the entrance
between rows of tall red pillars. The walls are of massive white – washed
stone with no windows in the lower storey. Just below the roof is a broad
band of dark red colour, and on top are tall shining gold ornaments and
small golden canopies. The houses for monks, three storeys high, are
crowded close together with narrow sandy lanes in between. About
seven thousand monks lived there, so it was really like a busy town.

The monastery was divided into three colleges, or *Tratsang*, each
of which was made up of several sub – colleges called *Khamtsen*. In
every Khamtsen there was at least one incarnate Lama who had his
own establishment known as a *Labrang*. These Labrangs were more
or less independent of the Khamtsen and some of them were very rich.
The Lamas had their own dwelling houses and private chapels in the
monastery; they owned estates in different parts of Tibet, and they had
their private household of attendants and servants. Although each
Labrang is connected with a particular Khamtsen, the Lama's household
are registered as members of his Labrang and do not come under the
control of the Abbot who is head of the Khamtsen. So I was enrolled
as a novice of the Sharpa Labrang, attached to the Kongbo Khamtsen
of the Me College of Sera.

I lived in Dote Chandzo's rooms, which were comfortable and
well – furnished. There were several other monks living there, too, either
Dote's attendants or those of the Lama. Sharpa Lama had given special
instructions that the Chandzo should look after me, so he did everything
for me himself. He washed and dressed me, fed me, and took me with

him every morning to the assembly in the principal hall of the monastery. There I sat beside him on his cushioned seat, rather like a little lap – dog, I suppose.

I can't remember much of this time. My earliest memories of the Labrang are being taken to the Lama's rooms most afternoons when he used to play with me, make me sing and dance for him, talk to me a little about religion and teach me simple prayers, and — later — to read and write. Apart from that I got no sort of education. The Lama was then about forty years old, I should think, and had a great reputation as a teacher. His special pupils came to him every morning, but I was too young for teaching of that sort. None of the other monks paid any attention to me and Dote Chandzo was far too busy with his administrative work. I think of him with gratitude, but without any real feeling. He was gentle and patient but showed no deeper interest in me. I was, after all, simply being looked after because that was the wish of his master, the Lama. For me the Lama was a second father and I remember him always with deep affection.

My mother came to see me whenever she could, bringing presents of butter, flour and delicacies. We met in the guest room of the Labrang for it would not have been proper for a woman to come to the Treasurer's rooms simply for a social visit, or to enter the Lama's own room except on a ceremonial occasion. Of course, with all the work of the house and farm, not to speak of the long journey, she could not come as often as she would have liked. My father came much more rarely; always at the New Year, and also at the end of the summer when there was a performance in the Khamtsen of the dramatic dances called Ache Lhamo. The monks always enjoyed entertaining their relations then, and took a lot of trouble to give them good food and look after them in every way. My parents sometimes stayed at that time in one of the small houses outside the monastery walls, where lay servants and shopkeepers lived. They always brought specially fine flour as a present for the Lama when they came.

My father had an elder brother who was a monk in another college of Sera. He was very learned, and much in demand as a teacher, so he had comfortable rooms and was well looked after by his pupils. They came to stay with him in turn, and made tea and so on for him, and kept his rooms clean. My father always went to see him, and I could visit him from time to time. He was kind and generous and gave me money, sweets and plenty of good advice.

It may seem a difficult life for a small boy to be parted from his home in that way; but it used to happen to many little Tibetans and, perhaps because the experience is shared by so many, it is not taken too tragically. We Tibetans seem to be rather tolerant and patient and it may be that the family bond is not so intense as in some other countries. Although I felt great love for my mother, I don't remember ever being unhappy in the Labrang — at least not for long. The Lama was kind and I lived in greater comfort than I would have done at home. It was boring sometimes, sitting in the Lama's room while he was talking to other people, so now and then I slipped out to play with other little monks. The Lama would scold me a little and slap me gently, when I came back, to teach me to be obedient and good mannered.

Once when Mother had brought me a jug of curds, of which I was very fond, I wanted to eat it at once; but the Lama took it from me and put it on top of a cupboard, saying I must wait until mealtime. I was very cross and I remember gazing up at the jug and howling miserably. Another time something must have upset me badly and made me feel neglected. I made up my mind to go home at once, and I set out alone from the monastery. I was still very small, and got no further than the sandy plain just outside the gates when someone found me and took me back to the Labrang. I was not scolded but was comforted and made happy again.

I remember one evening when I was with the Lama there was a strange noise in the sky. We hurried on to the roof and heard a drumming sound over our heads and saw lights flashing. I was rather frightened but the Lama said it must be an aeroplane. Later we heard that an aeroplane had crashed in the Tsang – po valley south of Lhasa and that some foreigners who were in it had been brought to the city. I saw them one day, wearing thick leather coats.

Another thing I remember from those early days is the excitement of going to bed on the eve of the New Year, knowing that there would be a surprise waiting for me next morning. Of course, I would wake up much too early and feel about for the presents I had been given, which were usually new clothes. It was rather like children here with their Christmas stockings.

One year the Lama went on a pilgrimage to a holy lake and as I was still too small to be taken on a long journey, I was allowed to go home for a month or so.

That as a very happy time. We used to get up quite early and have some tea and *tsampa*. Then the dogs were fed and the horses and donkeys taken out for their day's work. If there was a chance to ride one of the donkeys, I enjoyed that best. In the village I was allowed to wear layman's dress : trousers and a long, loose – fitting sort of coat belted up at the waist into a big pouch. My clothes were of red homespun to show that I was a monk but there was nothing to stop me playing with the village children all day. We would make mud houses, or dam the irrigation channels, watch the cows being milked, collect dung for fuel, or gather a black root like a truffle, which was very tasty. There was always plenty to eat. A pot of soup stood on the stove all day. I would find the hens' nests and take an egg to suck, or take a handful of parched barley grains out of the store bag, or take some mustard oil from the jar when mother wasn't looking. One day she caught me and picked up a big knife saying· she was going to cut off my hand. I wasn't frightened but my sister thought she meant it and cried loudly.

The main meal at home was at midday when we had *tsampa*, potatoes, cheese, and sometimes meat. One day I was hurling stones at a crane with my sling, in order to make it fly, when I hit it, by chance, on the head and killed it. I was ashamed and sorry because cranes are auspicious birds. I knew my father would be angry, because he was very religious – minded. I wanted to bury it but my sister made me take it home. She cooked it, stuffed with herbs and *tsampa*, and it was delicious. Sometimes we children caught partridges in horsehair snares, and they were good eating too. Our parents didn't really like us doing this but they could not resist eating what we had caught. In any case, it didn't matter so much about partridges because they are bad birds and if one sits on the roof of a house or comes into the yard, that is a sure sign of bad luck.

We had lots of stories about birds. The raven is very wise and clever and can foretell the future if you listen carefully to the different tones of its voice. But even the raven has to give way to the cuckoo, which is the king of birds. When the cuckoo arrives at Lhasa in spring, the ravens must leave the trees where they roost at night and go and perch on the rocks. But the cuckoo is rather a bully and nips off the heads of little birds if they try to eat before it has had all it wants. Only the wren is not afraid. If we found an empty wren's nest we would throw it into a stream for, if you were lucky, a magic stick then came floating upstream and once you had it you could make yourself invisible when you wanted. The chough is a good bird and is one of the attendants of Kongtsun Demo, the deity who protects Kongbo Khamtsen to which I belonged. But the jackdaw is bad because it disobeyed orders when the Chinese Princess was building the Ramoche temple — it did not bring wood as it was asked, so it is not allowed to come to Lhasa. The magpie is bad, too, because the young ones kill their mother.

I used to hear all those stories when we sat round after the evening meal. That meal was often quite late, and after it the women would clean and sort wool and the men would spin it, or perhaps make boot – soles out of hemp or do other jobs. The only light we had was from small lamps with a wick in mustard oil. It was quite good enough, for no one could read and instead we used to sing or tell stories. When it was time for bed we just unrolled our blankets. My father would take a small pot of *chang* to put beside his bed. Most Tibetan men have this "bed – chang" which is always the best quality, and some noble families usually have it sweetened.

I went home from the monastery several times after that; but that was the first visit I remember, and the happiest.

III
HAPPY DAYS AS A YOUNG NOVICE

As I grew older and was able to fend for myself, I was sent to take my place at the morning assembly along with the other novices. I suppose the great hall could hold about 5,000 people, but attendance was not really compulsory and the whole population of Sera was probably never there at one and the same time. The poorer monks went regularly because of the meal of barley gruel that was served. On special occasions there would be rice and meat, also a distribution of money when some devout patron acted as almsgiver. There were always large crowds then. But monks who could afford to buy their own food did not need to go every day, and I am afraid I only went when it was known that there was to be a good distribution of alms and of special food.

The assembly was about 7 or 9 a.m. according to the time of year. It was summoned by a time – keeper who went up on to the roof of the hall at dawn and kept on, for about three hours, intoning "Om Swasti" at regular intervals. After six such calls he hit one of the tall gold, cylindrical, ornaments on the roof which rang like a gong. The same sort of thing was done at the other great monasteries but there were different calls: at Drepung the time – keeper shouted "Chip, Chip" which means "Come!...Come!; and at Ganden he beat a drum. It was tiring work as the monk who did it had to be there winter and summer. He was also responsible during the day for keeping dogs out of the courtyard of the assembly hall, so he got special allowances of flour and butter.

Towards the end of the calling, the monks gathered on the wide stone steps until the doors were opened. This was done after the last call, which was followed by a blast on a conch shell trumpet. Then there was a rush for places. The Abbots, Incarnate Lamas and monastery officials had their own seats on thrones up by the altars. Senior monks, by custom, took their places at the head of the rows of dark red, rather greasy, padded mats stretching the whole length of the hall between a regular forest of great wooden pillars wrapped in red cloth. The rest of the monks just sat where they could. The smaller ones naturally kept back to avoid being crushed in the scramble. Some did not manage to get in at all before the door was locked.

The hall was dark and smelt heavily of incense and old butter. At the back of it, in a series of chapels and altars, were many large and beautiful gilded images, draped in brocade robes, with huge golden butter – lamps and all sorts of offerings and religious symbols in front of them. The walls were covered with frescoes of religious scenes, and painted banners and silken streamers hung from the pillars.

The prayer service for which we had assembled was accompanied at intervals by oboes, drums and handbells. I joined in the chanting when I had learnt the prayers by heart; but it was not always a serious occasion for the little monks, who often managed to squat down in the gap between two rows of seats. There they would joke and squabble if they could escape the notice of the proctors, who stalked up and down to keep order, and would lash out with a stout stick at the head and shoulders of anyone they caught not behaving properly. Another of the little monks' tricks was to try to get a distribution of alms in each of the rows between which they were hiding.

After the assembly the learned monks went to classes in their own colleges or to study and meditate in their cells. About midday each college held an assembly in its own hall. That was better attended than the general assembly in the morning, because the food was supposed to be better and we were given plenty of tea. The arrangements were much the same as in the great hall, but there was no rush for places as we had to go in quietly, and in a regular order. There was another service in the great hall in the afternoon. A last service was held in our own *khamtsen* about 8 in the evening, after which we were expected to go to bed or, at least, to our own rooms. In fact, ordinary little monks like myself usually went to play somewhere. I had four or five special friends, mostly from Kongbo Khamtsen with whom I used to share the extra *tsampa* I got from home and from the Labrang, which was rich compared with the khamtsen. We would go off to the kitchen and play knuckle – bones or a sort of draughts until some senior monk drove us off to bed.

It was clear enough that I was not going to be a learned monk — a *pe – cha – wa* or "bookman" as we called them. That was very much my own inclination, but really there was little choice because novices in a Labrang are taken on mainly to be useful about the place. They only get a religious training if they or their parents make a considerable effort to look for and to pay a teacher. That was one reason why my father had not liked my going to a Labrang. He would gladly have paid for me to be taught, but the Lama was officially my teacher and I could not have looked for anyone else. He probably intended to have taught me later on, if things had turned out differently.

In fact, a large number of monks got through their whole life without any systematic teaching. Some just did not want to learn when they were young; others might not have the money or family connections to find a religious tutor easily, for something has to be paid when a pupil is accepted, and most teachers will only take on a few pupils. But a boy who was really determined to learn could somehow find a teacher, perhaps by acting as a servant or by borrowing money. It happened sometimes that monks who had been unwilling to make an effort of that sort, and who had spent their early life as illiterates, would begin to study seriously when they were older, even as old as forty or so, when they had made a little money. Others might withdraw from the world into religious meditation. There were some little novices who lived outside the monastery. They were usually from very poor families who got permission for the boys to come into the monastery to work in the kitchens or stables and to get their food. Most of the boys simply disappeared when they grew up and got work as laymen. Some were allowed to enrol as ordinary monks after five years or so; but they remained different in many ways. They never learnt the prayers nor the ways of behaviour — how to walk and to wear the robes properly — that other monks learn. They really came only to fill their stomachs and the name *Tolenpa* by which they were known implies just that.

Although I got no regular instruction I began to be given a few odd jobs around the Labrang and also to see something of the world outside the monastery. I would clean the Lama's room and hold a basin of water for him to wash in while his other attendants helped him to dress in the morning. Sometimes I was sent on messages in the Labrang. One day I was given the key of the steward's store and sent to get some butter. When I unlocked the door of the rather dark cellar I saw, right in front of me, two little boys playing on the floor. They were wearing white clothes, short trousers and a sort of jacket with short sleeves, and their hair was cut in a round fringe. I was terribly frightened and my hair stood on end.

I ran away without getting the butter, and told Dote Chandzo. He did not seem much surprised and said they were spirits who were often seen there in different forms. Another time, outside the Labrang chapel, I saw a beautifully dressed girl passing by. When I told my friends they said I was talking nonsense; but Dote Chandzo said it must have been Kongtsun Demo, our protecting deity. She looked kind and lovely, but there were other protectors who were very fierce and terrifying. There was a painting of one of them, with a head like a raven, which was kept covered up and only shown once a year.

Shappa Lama belonged to the house of Shatra, one of the leading families in Lhasa, and he often went to visit his noble friends and his relations in the city, especially the Shasur family which is a branch of Shatra. He usually took me with him, for it was customary for high Lamas to be accompanied by favourite personal attendants, known by the pleasant description of Chense — the Light of the Eye. I suppose I might have grown up to be a useful attendant to him, but at that time I was a sort of mixture of a pet and jester. I am told I was quite comic; and when we went to the great houses I would be made to sing and dance to amuse the host and guest. Shasur Teji, the head of the Shasur house, who was a high official and famous scholar was always very kind to me both then and later.

My friends used to tease me sometimes on these outings. Once when we were visiting the Abbot of the Medical School on the Chakpori hill, just opposite the Potala, I saw a monkey for the first time. It was a fine big one that the Abbot kept as a pet. It was sitting on a platform on top of a pole in the sunny courtyard of the Abbots house, which was a pleasant sheltered place with peach trees growing against the warm rock of the hillside. Someone told me to give my shawl to the monkey which, he said, would catch any fleas or lice there might be in it. I didn't think there were any but, for a joke, I handed my shawl to the monkey. It began picking at it and then gave me a look and began to tear it up. I was very angry and picked up a stick and ran at the monkey and hit it. It was just as angry as I was and almost as big. It jumped down and caught hold of me and bit my calf. I yelled with pain and fright until the Abbot's servants hurried to the rescue. I took care never to go near that monkey again, and the marks of its teeth were on my right leg until I lost it.

One house it was a particular treat to visit was that of Lhalu. Its mistress, the Lhalu Lhacham, was a very great lady of the oldest family in Tibet, the Lhagyari. She had married into the wealthy Lhalu family, in which two Dalai Lamas had been born, but her husband had died some time ago. The house was a little way outside the city, in a peaceful park of willow and poplar trees near a marshy lake full of water – birds. One building, where the two Dalai Lamas of the Lhalu family had stayed, and which the last Dalai Lama visited sometimes, was kept as a chapel full of magnificent images and gold and silver ritual vessels. Underneath it were underground passages and a stream of clear, sweet, water. It was always said that this water made the best barley – beer in Lhasa. In another part of the grounds was a little lake, surrounded by trees, with a small island in its middle. There was a graceful pavilion on the island, and we used to be entertained there and given the most lavish and delicious food.

Lhalu Lhacham was a stout, large person. She was always perfectly dressed in the formal clothes of a great lady, including a heavy headdress covered in precious coral and pearls. She liked Sharpa Lama, and was greatly amused by me and made a great fuss of me, and kept stuffing sweets and good things into the front of my robe. She was full of jokes and amusing talk but was always unmistakably a great and dignified lady. It was well known in Lhasa that other noble ladies, and most of the noblemen, too, regarded her with awe and respect. Her servants, who were all good – looking and smartly dressed, were devoted to her and she knew all about their families and treated them with real kindness. She took such a liking to me that she would ask me to visit her even when the Lama could not go. A horse and servant would be sent to fetch me, and we would have lunch together with only her little grand-daughter and perhaps some other children there. I remember going when I was so small that I needed extra cushions to reach the table. After lunch we children played together — there was a toy bicycle with which we had great fun.

The Lhacham had so genuine an interest in even a small village boy like me that she asked my father to visit her, and received him with her natural kindness and sent him home with a generous present. Hers was an exceptional household. In others where I went I was treated kindly, but nowhere else was I so happy or so much at home as at Lhalu.

That rather pampered life did not last long. When I was about nine my Lama died. He had been ill for a little time and went to Shasur house in Lhasa for treatment. But he did not improve and his body swelled up with dropsy. Not long before he died he asked a venerable old Lama to visit him and they talked and meditated together for a very long time, after which my Lama was peaceful in his mind and quite ready to die. I was with him in Shasur house and his death made me terribly sad, but we had been taught to think of death as nothing very important; it is just one stage in all the births and deaths each of us has to go through. There should be even less sorrow for an incarnate Lama, because he has chosen to come back to the world to help other people find their deliverance, and he must have chosen his time to leave it. It was expected that my Lama would come back again in the body of a small child, to continue his work. Still, I missed him bitterly. He had been kind and affectionate and had treated me like a son. His body was carried from Lhasa in a long procession of many Lamas, monks and nobles, back to the hermitage above Sera where I had first been taken to him; and there it was cremated.

IV
STABLE HAND

Dote Chandzo took me back to his rooms and comforted me as well as he could. I stayed with him for some time, but it did not take me long to realize that I had lost my special position and was now just a very ordinary novice. Before long I moved from the Chandzo's rooms into the kitchen or the stables. There was nowhere else to stay in the Labrang, for there were no private rooms here for monks as there were in the colleges.

Soon after the Lama's death, Shasur Teji sent four young men from his estates to be novices in the Labrang. It had become rather short-handed and as he had a family connection with it because of the late Lama, he sent these youths. They were about 16 to 18 years old and had been to school in Lhasa. They did not want to become monks but had to do as they were told. Like me, they were not taught religion but were kept simply as helpers around the Labrang and its estates. It was the rule that newly joined monks should show respect to those who have been monks for a longer time; but as the new novices were so much older than me they tried to impose on me and make me do all the dirty work. When I was angry with them and said they should treat me with respect, they only laughed. I wanted to complain to Shasur Teji but the Chandzo persuaded me not to, though he did not do much himself to help me.

Now I really had to do a lot of hard work. The Labrang had a number of horses. I had enjoyed riding them when the Lama was alive; but now I had to look after them as little more than a stable hand. I cleaned out the stable, groomed the horses, took them to water and so on. I soon got used to it and as I liked horses it was not too bad. There was one very tall, strong, roan from the Kokonor country of which I was particularly fond and I used to ride him every day when I drove the other horses to water. I could not get on his back without help but was quite at home once I was mounted, and it was great fun galloping along bareback shouting at the other horses and rounding them up. As I was very small and the horse unusually big and handsome, we were soon noticed by other people and I got a nickname meaning "Sharpa Labrang's monkey - on - horseback". The name comes from a favourite picture of four animal friends -- an elephant, a monkey, a hare, and a parrot. The monkey is shown sitting on the elephants back, the hare on the monkey's back and the parrot perched on top of the hare.

My Lama had had a favourite horse which was very sleek and strong; but after his master died he refused to eat and it looked as if he would die too. So he was sent off to graze in the valley of Phenpo and we supposed that was the last of him. Women and children there rode him sometimes or made him carry loads of wood but he was so weak that he could only struggle along. The strange thing is that when the new incarnation of my Lama was discovered a few years later, the horse suddenly recovered and became strong and sleek again. He was brought back to the Labrang and the little child in whose body my master, Sharpa Lama, had come back to earth rode the horse for several years after. The new Lama was discovered in the noble family of Rampa whose head was the monk minister in the Tibetan Cabinet. He was very fond of me, just as though he remembered me.

Not long after my Lama's death there was a great excitement and disturbance in Sera. It was caused by a serious difference between the Government and the Lama of Reting, who had been Regent of Tibet from the death of the XIIIth Dalai Lama until about 1941. At that time, I am told, he became rather unpopular with the monks of the other great monasteries and he retired. It seems that he expected to be asked to come back after a few years. When this did not happen, his friends began to intrigue against his successor, planning to restore the Reting Lama as Regent by force. The Reting Lama was connected with the Che college of Sera, which had many monks from East Tibet, and it was said that he was trying to get help from the Chinese through them. I don't really know the facts. I was too young to take in exactly what was going on and, in any case, many of the rumours we heard in the monastery were probably not true.

At all events, one evening there was a buzz of activity in Che and a special religious ceremony was held. Next morning we saw the Che monks wearing lay dress and armed with all sorts of weapons, rifles, swords, and spears, pouring out of the monastery and up into hills behind it, and into the ravines and little woods nearby. Then we heard that the Reting Lama had been arrested in his own monastery, some three days march from Lhasa, and was being brought to the capital, accused of plotting against the Government.

The story we heard later was that a carefully sealed parcel had been delivered to the Regent's Secretary with a message that it should be given into the Regent's own hands. When one of the Secretary's servants was opening it, it exploded, wounding the man very badly. After a careful enquiry, it appeared that a cousin of the Reting Lama and a clever young Lama from East Tibet who was connected with Sera Che, together with some others, including the young and much respected Lama of Karto, a small monastery on a hill near Sera, had been responsible. The young Lama of Sera Che, who was very clever with his hands, was said to have made the exploding box. They were arrested, and a Cabinet Minister went to Reting with some troops to arrest the former Regent as well. We heard later that the Minister did not dare to let the Reting Lama ride his own horse which was so famous for strength and speed. They were afraid that once he got on it he might escape; so he was made to ride a mule.

When the monks of Che heard about the arrests, they decided they would rescue the Reting Lama. They went quite wild and even killed their Abbot when he tried to restrain them. On the morning when we saw them rushing out of their college, they were preparing to intercept the party bringing the Reting Lama to Lhasa under arrest. As soon as the Tibetan troops came in sight, the monks opened fire on them. While great harm was done, they did not succeed in rescuing the Lama; but this was the start of all sorts of disturbances in and around Lhasa. Some of the Che monks went into the city by night to stir up trouble, and there was occasional shooting.

We in Me college were called together by our Abbot and told that this was no business of ours and we must stay in our Khamtsen and keep quiet. In the meantime Che was almost empty. Only very old monks and the servants stayed there. The cooks made food every day and took it out to the monks in their positions on the hills. There was much excited talk and coming and going. In the meantime the trial of the prisoners was being held in the National Assembly. We heard that the Reting Lama denied having plotted against the Government, but that the others had confessed. The Che monks refused to accept this and would not return to their college. Eventually the Government warned them that unless they gave up their threatening behaviour they would be attacked.

Mountain guns were now brought up near the Trapchi barracks not far from Sera and one morning, about then days after the start of the trouble, the guns opened fire. When the shells crashed into the buildings of Che we were frightened and took cover wherever we could; but the shooting was accurate and no shell landed near our college. In fact, when any of our monks wanted to go out of the monastery he would wave his shawl over his head and the soldiers would let him go past safely. A good deal of damage was done to the buildings of Che college, but as there were so few people left there, no one was hurt. It was very different on the hills and in the ditches around the monastery where the Che monks were holding their positions. They even had a large home-made cannon which they loaded with all sorts of metal fragments and let off with an enormous bang. After firing it they rushed the old cannon back into shelter and loaded it again. That took a long time, but they claimed that they killed a lot of soldiers in the barracks. On their side they lost many men, and were eventually driven from the hills. Many of them escaped to distant parts of the country and some went to China.

After the fighting was over I went up the hillside with some friends. It was terrible to see the bodies lying there. Many had been rolled together into the ravines, and some of the soldiers and poor people of Lhasa had been there and stripped them of everything worth taking. They got quite a haul of swords, daggers, snuff bottles, brocade waistcoats and so on. I picked up what looked like a good blanket I saw lying by a rock but I found it had a man's leg wrapped in it and was covered in blood. However, my friends and I collected a great many empty cartridge cases which we took to Lhasa and sold to the metal workers. As there were few people left in Che to look after the dead, most of the bodies were buried in the sandy ground near the barracks instead of being properly cut up and given to the dogs and vultures. Because of this neglect, the spirits of some of the dead monks became restless demons and for a long time we used to hear their shrill shouts of "Ki hu hu !" echoing on the hills at night.

Not long after, the Reting Lama died in confinement in the Potala. It was said that he was so full of remorse for what had happened that he did not want to live. Other people said he had been murdered. I don't know what was the truth. The Lama's cousin and Lama of Karto were sentenced to imprisonment for life, and a special prison house was built for them in the barracks of the Dalai Lama's Bodyguard Regiment. First they were flogged and this seemed a terribly sad thing to many people in Lhasa, especially as the Karto Lama had been very popular. I saw him one day in Lhasa after the trial, wearing a wooden yoke on his neck. The women all round were weeping and lamenting. Some of the Sera Che monks who had taken a leading part were captured. They were handed over to leading households of Lhasa which were made responsible for their safe - keeping and good behaviour. The prisoners wore light chains round their legs but were well treated by their keepers.

After the excitement had died down I found myself becoming more and more dissatisfied with being nothing better than a stable boy. I was growing up and wanted something interesting to do. I don't want to give the impression that I was actually unhappy but, having been a favourite and rather spoiled, it was a change to be no one in particular. I got on well enough with my companions and began to be friendly with Tashi Tsering, who had a room of his own in Kingbo Khamtsen. He was a bookman and quite clever, but rather poor. He worked with a teacher, and used to go to his room about twice a week. He would stay there and look after his teacher as well as getting religious instruction. When he was at home, he usually read for about two hours every morning and then got down to making clothers for other monks. He did this very well and so it brought him enough money to pay his teacher. I went to stay with him, which was a very pleasant change from the Labrang kitchen. A lot of other monks used to go to Lhasa almost every day; but unless one had money to spend there was not much point doing that, so Tashi Tsering and I usually stayed around the monastery and sometimes walked in the willow groves nearby. He used to advise me to find a teacher; and my uncle gave me the same advice whenever I went to see him. But I was not interested and all I wanted was to be able to join a special class of monks called *dob dob* about whom I shall have a lot to say later. I was still too young for that but I used to dream about it, particularly about the smart clothes they wore and the sports they practised and the dashing way they behaved. In the meantime I just had to wait.

I often asked Dote Chandzo to find me some other work to do

or else let me go home. He was always patient and said he would see about it; but as nothing changed, I decided I would just go off home for a time. By now I was quite able to take care of myself. I soon found a man with some donkeys going the right direction and when I asked to join his party he let me ride a donkey all the way.

When my parents heard why I had come, Mother made a great fuss over me, and Father was quite sympathetic but he said I must go back and he would see what could be done for me. At any rate, he said, I should stay at home for a few days. However, before long a monk from the Labrang came to our house looking for me. I had not asked permission to leave, so when Dote Chandzo heard that I was missing he guessed where I had gone and sent the monk to bring me back. He was a surly fellow I did not know well, and he told me to start off at once. So we set off on the road; he was riding and I was walking. Almost as soon as we had left the house he told me to pick up a big stone and carry it on my back as a punishment. My father had been watching and when he saw this he hurried after us and spoke to the monk with more anger than I had ever seen him show. I think he even gave the monk a push which was a daring thing for a farmer to do. He said he had not sent his son to Sera to be treated harshly, and that he would not let me go any further with the monk but would bring me back himself and talk to the Chandzo. So the monk rode off scowling and I went back home.

I was allowed a few happy weeks with my family and then Mother took me on horseback to the Labrang and had a discussion with Dote Chandzo. She told him that my parents had not expected that I should be just a Labrang servant and that I might as well work at home and help my family. He was not at all annoyed,although, I suppose, he found me rather a nuisance. He said he would see about taking me with him to one of the Labrang's estates when he went later in the year Soon after, he told me we would go to Dangpo, a district about ninety miles from Lhasa, where one of his relations was steward of an estate which had a large herd of yaks.

I could hardly wait for that new experience. But before the time came I had a short change from my stable work, when I was chosen to take part in a ceremony called Tsomcho Serpang. I was to join in a grand procession from the Jokhang -- the Cathedral of Lhasa -- all round the Potala. Monks from most monasteries take part and I was part of the representation from Sera.

The head of our Khamtsen had told me and the others to get our heads cleanly shaven a day or so before; and on the morning of the ceremony we got up very early, washed our faces and arms well, put on our best clothes, and went to the Jokhang. There the custodians were handing out a great collection of sacred treasures, one to each monk, to carry in the procession. There were conch shells decorated with heavy gold and silver ornaments, old musical instruments, holy water jugs and vases, pictures, images and many other things. I carried a cylindrical silk banner on a tall thin stick. There were eight or nine of us with such banners.

The whole procession was several hundred strong. It included the elephant belonging to the Dalai Lama, also the cardboard figure of another elephant carried by several men, and tall images of the Guardians of the Four Quarters supported on the shoulders of specially strong monks. It took a long time to get everything arranged in the proper order but we set out as soon as the sun was up. At the same time an enormous embroidered hanging, with pictures of the Buddha and Saints worked on it, was hauled up and spead over the lower face of the Potala. It must have been about 80 feet high and even wider.

We moved along very slowly with long halts at different places, and a very long interval when some parts of the procession went into the enclosure at the foot of the Potala to be seen by the Dalai Lama from a window of the Palace and by the Cabinet who were in a tent down below. The elephant driver, who was dressed as an Indian, shouted Accha Salaam at the top of his voice and made the elephant salute the Dalai Lama. Then there were different groups of dancers, including a party of particularly strong young monks from Gongkar monastery, who danced with heavy drums on their backs which they beat behind them with long - handled sticks. That was a very vigorous and strenuous dance and needed a lot of practice and physical training. The dancers got a special allowance of rice and tea. In fact they were the only people in the procession to be given food. The story is that long ago the Fifth Dalai Lama was watching them when he saw one of the dancers dropping balls of tsampa out of his pouch, so he realized that if they had to bring food with them, it must be very hard work. He ordered them to be given rice and tea and it has been done ever since.

A group of four learned monks performed a salute to the Dalai Lama in very slow motion, raising their hands, almost imperciptibly, to their yellow hats, taking them off equally slowly, unwrapping their cloaks of red and yellow -- a special sort you see in old paintings and supposed to come from India -- then sinking slowly to their knees and prostrating themselves very, very slowly.

After that the Nechung Oracle rushed out of a building below the Potala in a state of possession and danced wildly in front of the Cabinet, who gave him scarves and received his blessing.

During these performances a jester, supposed to be an Indian cowherd, wenting about in the crowd. He came along with a cow and a pail into which he pretended to milk it; and he played all sorts of tricks to amuse the people. Every year a *dob dob* monk of Sera was chosen by the Proctors to play this part, and it was quite sought after because the people gave him money and he was allowed to go round the houses in the city to do his tricks and get various little rewards. He had to wear a special mask, which was believed to be very sacred and was kept in the Potala. For some reason, the inside of it was covered with dried blood. The monk who was chosen to wear it had to live a pure life and be very careful to keep clean for a month before the ceremony. One year the chosen man seems to have got into trouble of some sort and failed to keep the rules. The mask shrank so much that he could not get it on, so he was disgraced.

When the ceremonies in the courtyard were finished, the procession moved on slowly through the chorten gate at the foot of the Potala hill, all round the hill itself and, so gradually, back to the Jokhang, where all the treasures were carefully taken back by the custodians and examined to see that they had suffered no damage. It was late before the whole thing was over. It was a tiring day with so much standing about and not much to eat except what we could bring with us.

V
TWO YEARS IN THE MOUNTAINS OF DAGPO

It was late autumn before the head herdsman came from the *drok* -- which is Tibetan for the grazing land -- bringing the year's produce of butter and cheese for the Labrang. He was to accompany Dote Chandzo and me back to Dagpo. I was impatient to start at once. Tshapanang was the furthest I had been, and now I was eager to see new places and new ways. The herdmaster naturally wanted time to visit the holy places and do his own marketing; but at last everything was ready and we set out on our journey which was to take six or seven days.

We were all on horseback and driving the pack - yaks, which had loads of flour and grain for the return trip. That meant it was rather slow going, because yaks can't be hurried; but it was good travelling weather; dry, clear and sunny, without much wind. I enjoyed every minute and felt very free.

The first couple of days took us up the valley of the Kyi river then we turned up a side valley and began to climb up gradually, crossing a high pass most days and spending the nights in villages which were much simpler and poorer than Tshapanang. Finally we came down through high grazing grounds to the winter quarters where the herds of yak were just beginning to gather. This was Drilung Shika, centring round an estate house belonging to Sharpa Labrang, not far from the district governor's headquarters in the castle of Oka. The herds were out on some grassy slopes a little way from the house, and the herdsmen had pitched their black tents there. At first I was taken with Dote Chandzo to stay in the estate house with his relation, the steward, who was a young layman with a wife and family. The house was very tall and strongly built, standing in a fine grove of ancient willows with huge twisted trunks. There is a special enclosure there with good rooms set aside for the Dalai Lama to stay in whenever he visits the place on his way to the famous sacred eake of Chokhorgye three days further up the valley.

The lake is high up in the mountains and can only be reached by yak or on foot. Lamas go there to look in the water in the hope of seeing visions of the future. The present Dalai Lama was discovered after the Reting Lama had visited the lake and had seen on its calm surface a vision of a house with gilt pinnacles, and fir trees beside it. There were other signs too which were later found, exactly as he had seen them, marking the house where the Dalai Lama was born. The present incarnation of the Sharpa Lama was also found after a lama had seen the Rampa house, quite clearly, in the lake. I am sorry I never managed to go there although I met a lot of pilgrims on their way up and down in the autumn.

There are some fine hot springs near Drilung Shika, very good for rheumatism and such troubles. One of them is kept specially for the Dalai Lama. Soon after we reached the *drok* we went for a picnic there and enjoyed bathing in the hot water.

While I stayed in the estate house I went most days to visit the herdsmen to get to know them and find out about the work. It was important, too, that their dogs should get to know me otherwise I might have been torn to bits. These herd - dogs are very strong and fierce. One kind is big and heavy with a huge head, thick hairy coat and brown patches over its eyes. Dogs of that size usually stay tied up in the camp as watch dogs. Rather smaller dogs. much the same to look at, go out with the herdsmen, and, as they are not so heavily built, they can travel great distances and chase wolves and other dangerous animals. They all have thick red woollen collars to protect their throats in a fight with wolves.

At this time I was wearing lay dress but was recognizable as a monk by its red colour and by my short hair. The herdsmen were very simple and friendly and, although they treated me with the formal deference due to a monk, I was quickly accepted as one of the family. There were two children in the family I joined, a boy and a girl both younger than me -- I suppose I was about 12 at the time -- but they did their work so easily, managing and riding the yaks, putting up tents, tying knots, controlling the dogs and so on, that I was quite envious; but I soon began to pick up those things.

I spent the New Year in the estate house. It was all very simple and happy, a great change from the crowd and fuss at Sera and the even greater crowd at the ceremonies in Lhasa. Monks came from a neighbouring monastery to recite prayers; then there was feasting, dancing, and singing, in which the herdsmen joined. Some of the people from the estate went to watch a religious dance at the monastery, but I had seen enough of that at Lhasa so I did not go. One day we went with presents and good wishes to the district governor. Then we exchanged parties with the people on neighbouring estates. There was no one very near, and when we went out it usually took half a day or more, sometimes riding on yaks.

In the second month, about the end of March, I went to live with the herdsmen in their black tents. I dressed now like them in a single sheepskin cloak with the fleece inside, and nothing else except homespun boots. It is a comfortable dress and I was never cold. The tents made of woven yak - hair were surprisingly warm and waterproof. The herdsmen made a low wall of turf round the sides to keep out draughts. Inside, although the roof was rather low, there was quite enough room for six or seven people. There was a carpet of felt on the floor, a small altar at the back, and, of course, a cooking stove always with a big copper cauldron on it right in the centre of the tent. The smoke from the fire of dry yak dung was troublesome at first but one soon got used to it. It did get a bit cold at night in winter, but there were plenty of thick blankets.

When the herdsmen knew from the signs of the season that it was time to leave winter quarters, we began to move the yaks upwards to the higher slopes where grass was beginning to grow. Our first camp after leaving Drilung Shika was near the little monastery of Samding. It is a lovely place on the slope of a sacred snow mountain, surrounded by juniper bushes, very quiet and peaceful. Deer and pheasants used to go quite fearlessly right into the courtyard of the monastery. There were four tents in our encampment here; the rest of the herdsmen who had been near Drilung Shika went off to other camps and we would not see them again until autumn.

My work with the other children was to look after the baby yaks which were being born on the slopes above our tent. The cows seemed to have very little trouble, dropping their calves very quickly, and the little things were very soon tottering on their feet. The herdsmen carried them down to the camp with the mothers grunting after them. A few days later, the calves were separated from the mothers, and we children had to take them to a separate slope out of sight of the place where their mothers were sent. The first few days were the hardest, as the calves were always struggling to get back to the tents where they though they would find their mothers. Even a baby yak is a handful for a boy or girl to manage. We made them collars and tied two or three of them together so that they would be a drag on one another for they never seemed to want to go the same way at the same time. They gradually got used to being kept apart, but until then it was hard work chasing after them, catching them and dragging them back. After that, it was less trouble, and the calves could be kept from straying by shouting or by hurling small stones at them from a sling. Another job we had to do quite early was to pierce holes in their noses to put a nose ring through later. When we did this we gave their names. And after a time we had to tie crossed sticks round their necks so that if they did manage to escape and find their mothers they would not be able to suck.

It was a wonderfully happy time up on the hills. We would play at making our own camps and visiting one another, or throw stones at a mark, and play many other games. Sometimes we caught bumblebees and stuck a yellow flower into their backsides and found it very funny to see them buzzing away with that decoration behind them. There was no shelter from rain, wind, or snow showers except behind some big boulder; but we had no worries and when it was sunny it was the finest possible life lying up there on the grass watching the little yaks grazing and playing round us. I would play the flute, which sounded very sweet, and echoed in the valleys. There was nothing else to hear except the yaks, and the trickle of water, and birds calling. Down below we could see, far away in the clear air, the black tents with blue smoke trickling out of them and a patch of lighter colour all round them where the cheeses were laid out to dry. We had roasted barley meal with us, and cheese, and often some dried meat too, and always a yak horn full of buttermilk. The days passed quietly and happily. I would tell the others stories of Sera and Lhasa, and they told me about their life and about the wild animals in the hills.

Towards evening the women in the camp lit incense in several great pots, and we saw the thick column of creamy smoke towering up. The calves usually saw it first and knew it was time to go home. They began to frisk and caper down towards the tents, tails in the air like flags, jumping on stiff legs and grunting with excitement. We scurried after them and got them into two lines, facing each other, and tied them up head to head. There they waited, tugging and grunting, for the next event. Very soon they could see and hear what was coming, for the man who was looking after the yak - cows on another hill now drove them down from the pasture. They came rushing home, pushing, jostling and lowing, with a great noise and dust. First they were driven into a pen where the women milked them. The calves were wild with impatience when they smelt the sweet milk. Then at last the cows were turned loose and we let the calves free. Every calf soon found its mother and sucked and butted away eagerly while the cow nuzzled it. When that was over the calves were tied up again, the cows driven into a pen for the night, and the dogs set on guard.

We were hungry for supper after all that. There was an abundance of good food: plenty of milk and butter, thick gruel of *tsampa* with cheese, and sometimes a delicious treat of barley flour mixed with blood drawn from the neck of one of the animals, which we toasted on sticks. We might sit about for a short time afterwards in the light of oil lamps or butter lamps, the women sewing or working with wool, the men making boot soles or headropes, and we children perhaps cutting wooden toggles to tighten the ropes. But we would soon roll up in our blankets and sleep.

The women got up early in the morning. First they lit incense outside the tents. Then they went to milk the yak cows again. They milked into wooden pails which had a willow twig twisted round the rim to prevent splashing. Drops of cream stuck to the twig and by scraping it off after a time, a rich cream cheese was collected.

The milk was poured into big vats lined up side by side in a trench with a wooden platform at the side on which the women stood and slowly churned the milk with wooden paddles, singing the churning song all the time. In a big camp you might see two rows of milk tubs in a wide trench with, perhaps, four men on one side and four women on the other, all churning away and singing the whole time. It was a great sight.

When the butter was ready, the mistress of the camp carefully washed her arm up to the elbow and plunged it into the tubs, collecting the butter with a sweeping motion. The butter was put into water in other tubs for a time and the buttermilk was poured into a huge copper cauldron over the fire; some whey was added and the cauldron left to simmer until cheese formed. This was a soft cheese and great quantities of it were made. Monks and other people from the neighbourhood used to come long distances to buy it, giving in exchange things like vegetables, oil, and barley; but there was always a very large supply to be taken later in the year to the Labrang, and for sale in the Lhasa market.

After a month or so near Samding monastery we moved our camp higher up the valley. At each site there were turf walls, inside which the tents were pitched; sometimes the walls had to be repaired, but the herdsmen never went to a new site. I suppose the places had originally been chosen carefully for shelter, and for supplies of water and fuel. The hillsides in that part of Dagpo were mostly well covered with juniper scrub and other bushes, and there were plenty of wild animals in the cover -- hares, foxes, deer, lynx, and the *drokpas* special enemies, wolves and leopards; there were also packs of wild dogs which were very fierce and destructive; they tried to drive their victims downhill and often into a stream where they would tear them to pieces. We used to hear them barking and calling sharply all the time, as though they were talking to one another, so I did not like to go far out on the hills at night. I made a clay whistle to blow, and sometimes I would shout out loudly to scare off any wolves, or the like, that might be about.

There were bears, too, in the hills. We call them "man - bear" or "dog - bear" and I think they must be what foreigners call the "Snowman". One of them was killed while I was with the herdsmen and I was able to have a good look at it. It was covered with tawny fur and had very square - shaped feet with long sharp claws. I noticed particularly that its face was much flatter than that of the ordinary bears that we saw lower down; it was almost as flat as a man's or a monkey's. The one that was killed was a huge male, and its body was certainly more like a bear's than a man's.

There are all sorts of stories about these bears. People say that they can ride a horse or a yak; and everyone knows that if you are chased by one you must run downhill because its hair falls over its face and it can't see where it is going. They can whistle like men, too; I know because I have heard them. There is a story of one female that caught a trader and kept him living with her for several years. The skins of the man - bears are much sought after. I have seen them quite often used by rich monks as bedcovers. They are quite different from great apes like gorillas and chimpanzees, which I have seen in zoos. We call those Mi - go, which means "wild man".

By the eighth month we had reached the furthest part of the

grazing grounds, high up in a hollow completely surrounded by mountains, and not far below the snow and ice. There were no more bushes and shrubs, but only rocks and close turf, with a few little flowers and a sweet - smelling plant, perhaps thyme. By then the nights were becoming quite cold and a strong wind began to blow in the afternoon; so it was clear that summer was coming to an end. The young yaks had grown fast. They had long since been wearned; but they got a good feed of buttermilk at night. I was quite an experienced yak - herd by now and had learnt all the skills from the herdsman's children.

Now we moved slowly down to Drilung Shika to spend the winter there. I stayed on with the herdsmen as I had become so used to a tent that I liked it better than the house. When we were down in winter quarters the young bulls were castrated, except for a few that were killed for meat. Only the master bull of a herd is left entire and it is not until he is growing old that another young bull is left to grow up; otherwise there would be terrible fights, for the herd bull is a huge, fierce and untameable beast and hardly anyone dares go near him. But the *drokpas* have a special custom of inviting the bull to their camp for the New Year.

The head herdsman goes off to look for the bull, taking a packet of salt and one of ashes. When he finds the bull, which may take a week or more, he offers the salt and ashes which are a great delicacy for yaks, and with this bait he gradually tempts the bull down to the camp where the rest of the herd is. A big bowl of barley beer is put down in the middle of a square enclosure and dishes of salt, ashes, grain, and flour are arranged at each corner. The bull is invited to come and drink; and when he does, the herdmaster takes a stick with a lump of butter on the end and tries to smear the butter on the bull's forehead right between the great horns. Everyone is careful not to annoy the bull and the rest of the herd all keep at a respectful distance. After he has drunk the beer he may stay around the camp for a few hours or even for a day or two and then he wanders off on his own, and probably will see no one again until the cows go up to the higher pastures in the summer, when he will mate with them.

For the herdsmen, that is the really important start to the New Year. After the bull's visit some monks are invited to the camp to hold a prayer service. Afterwards the herdsmen take their part in the usual New Year celebrations in the estate house, where they go to offer scarves and presents. Then they go the round of neighbouring camps, which might be quite far away, so it was arranged whose turn it was to wait at home to receive the guests. The leader of the visiting party rode a specially decorated yak and it had to be pure black with white horns. At this time the herdsmen kept all their dogs tied up well out of the way so that their visitors wouldn't have any trouble.

I spent another year with the herdsmen, much like the first only I was stronger and more experienced. When we were in our first camp we were visited by a party of Lopas from the forest country south of the mountains on the other side of the river. They are small people, with strong legs and big feet, who wear no clothes at all except for a small bamboo basket over their private parts; they also had rain cloaks of some sort of thick brown fibre. It seems they did not make either woollen or cotton cloth and hardly ever used such things, but they were very clever at working with bamboo and made beautiful mats and baskets. Although they do not speak Tibetan they were very friendly, and we talked through an interpreter they had brought to help them with their trading. They came to buy satt, butter and cheese, and such things as knives and bells if we had them to spare; and in exchange they offered bark for making red dye, musk, very strong and pleasant to smell, and deer horns in velvet which are used for medicine, especially by the Chinese. Those things brought a good profit in Lhasa. The Lopas are very clever hunters and we saw them shoot pigeons very accurately with their bows and arrows.

The biggest event of the year was a tremendous earthquake in the late summer. It was not long after dark. First the brass and copper ladles hanging on the tent wall began to rattle together. Then the whole earth shook and rumbled as if it was going to split open. There were loud explosions like cannon firing. Everyone was terrified; the yaks were stamping and struggling and the dogs howled miserably. People said that it was a war of the gods in the sky and must be a very bad omen. There had been rumours of a war with China, so we were afraid that something of the sort must be happening. In fact, the Chinese communists did attack East Tibet not long after; and that makes it possible to fix the date, which was 1950. When we got back to Drilung Shika at the beginning of winter we found that the upper stories of the house had collapsed and the ruined towers of the old fort at Oka had fallen. No one had been killed, but a cook who ran outside was buried in falling rubble and had to be dug out, rather badly hurt. Drilung was luckier than another drok not far away. The herdsmen were camping close under a glacier which came down on top of them and killed almost everyone, and a great many animals. The herd belonged to Sera and as soon as news reached there, supplies of food and clothes were sent out, and next year some new herdsmen and more animals were sent.

VI
NEW YEAR FESTIVAL AT LHASA

Soon after we had reached winter quarters, I heard that I had been sent for by the Labrang. I did not want to go back, as I was enjoying the free and happy life; but I had to obey, and when the head herdsman set out for Lhasa taking the year's supply of butter and cheese I went along with him. I had a fine big load of my own to take back, for while I was working with the *drokpas* I was given a big lump of butter every day as my wages. I had kept a great deal of that and had also collected a lot of cheese which I knew would be useful in Lhasa.

It was about a month before the New Year when we got back to the city. We found people there very worried and anxious. The Chinese had beaten our troops in East Tibet and captured the commander, the minister Ngapo. The Dalai Lama had left Lhasa for the Chumbi valley near India to wait there and see what would happen. Lhasa was full of rumours and alarms. Some of the monks were complaining that the soldiers had not fought well and that Ngapo wanted to give Tibet away, but we really did not know what had happened and were wondering whether the Chinese were on their way to attack Lhasa.

Before I went back to the Labrang I was allowed to visit my father and mother. It was a great happiness to see them again, and I was able to spend about a week at home. People in the village were much less disturbed and excited than in the city; and mother was delighted with all the butter and cheese I had brought for her.

When I went back to the monastery I stayed at first in the Labrang kitchen, as I had done before. My time with the *drokpas* had made me much tougher and more independent, besides I was growing up and the other novices didn't try to make me do all the work any more. It was much easier this time and I got on well with the others, who were eager to hear stories about life on the grazing grounds. I went to see my friends in Lhasa, especially the Shasur household. Shasur Teji said I should go to call on Lhalu Lhacham, but I was too shy to go to so great a lady now that I was no longer a child; so I never went.

Soon I made friends with a monk about my own age, called Sonam, who belonged to Kongbo Khamtsen but had hired a room for himself in another college because two of his brothers were there. We went together that year to attend the Great Prayer in Lhasa at the New Year. It was the third time I had attended it; Dote Chandzo had taken me when I was quite small. Sonam and I stayed in the temple of the Darpoling Oracle which was packed full of monks from Sera. We had to sleep with a lot of other young monks in the dark side - chapel of the protecting deities. It was rather a terrifying place, as the spirits that take possession of the Oracle's attendants are supposed to live there, and there were two big leather bags said to be full of the breath of dead persons. In one dark corner was an image of one of the deities, dressed in oracle's clothes and with chains round her ankles. Some of the boys said that the spirit used to walk about at night and go outside the chapel; they said they heard the sound of the chains dragging along. Some of them very bravely smeared fat on the images' feet and, sure enough, next morning the fat was all covered with dirt. We would not have dared to stay there if there had not been so many of us, and we took care to behave quietly and properly. All the same I did not much enjoy being there. But it was not so larming as the temple of another oracle, the Karmashar, which is the special oracle of Sera. A lot of Sera monks stay there at the New Year, but they never dare to go into the side chapel at night. There is a famous mask there which represents a former attendant of the oracle, called Ngawang Namgye, who had the power to leave his body at night and wander about like a spirit. When he died the mask was made to represent him. Quite often he is heard moving about the chapel and the mask is found in the morning to be covered with snuff, and smelling strongly of *chang*, both of which Ngawang Namgye used to like very much.

At all events, we did not spend much time in the Darpoling chapel, and Lhasa was an exciting and crowded place at the New Year. The Old Year ended with a ceremony of dancing to drive out the evil and sins of the year that was past. The greatest of these dances was performed in the western courtyard of the Potala, and the Dalai Lama watched it from his rooms high above the dancing place. There was a heavy gold cornice over his windows, which were veiled in gauze and hung with yellow curtains. The dancers were monks from his private monastery in The Potala and the dance lasted all day. The dances, masks and dresses have been described by foreign visitors and I have seen photographs of them in foreign books; but I only went there once myself because we had our own ceremoney at Sera. I went once, too, to Muru monastery where they have a very famous collection of old masks and dresses which can only be seen at the New Year dance.

The First two days of the year were holidays for us in the monasteries. Our families and friends, wearing their best clothes, came to visit us and to make a tour of the shrines and chapels. My parents usually came on the second day because they had to celebrate the first day in the village. There everyone got up very early and had a special sort of sour soup and a drink of barley beer; everyone had that, including the smallest children. Then people from every house would make the rounds of their friends carrying a tray of flour and barley from which everyone would take a pinch and scatter it in the air for good luck; and, of course, there was beer too, in a silver jug with butter on the spout. There would be burning of incense and singing of special songs. It was all very happy and gay. Everyone looked clean and smart; the men in fine broadcloth robes and white shirts, and round hats with ear flaps beautifully decorated with gold thread; the women put on bright silk blouses and their finest striped aprons, and wore their best ornaments -- coral - studded headdresses and silver charm - boxes set with turquoise. People would go to the monastery near the village and then spend the day in having parties.

The next day my father and mother would probably come to Sera where they hired a room in one of the small houses outside the monastery wall. They brought scarves and presents for me and a brass pail full of butter to fill the butter lamps in the chapels which they visited. They had lunch with me and with other parties of monks and their guests in the Labrang guest room. The monastery gave us pastry, tea and meat on that occasion and we were allowed to play games such as cards and dominoes, which were forbidden at all other times.

On the third day a stream of monks began to flow into Lhasa from all directions, looking for somewhere to stay. Some colleges and Khamtsen had houses of their own which would be packed with monks; others were entertained in private houses or shops, and it was thought to be a meritorious act to have a monk to stay in your house during the Great Prayer. Sonam and I went to Darpoling that year because it had an old connection with Sera.

The next day we went to reserve a place in the big assembly hall of the Jokhang -- the Cathedral of Lhasa. By custom the older monks got seats in the main body of the hall while the rest of us crowded in, all round and between the regular rows of seats and in any space or corner we could find. The proctors' assistants would tell us where it was all right for us to sit, and once we had found a place we would go back there every time we attended the assembly.

With so many monks crowding into Lhasa the monasteries were almost completely deserted, except for the sick and the old. Each college left two responsible watchmen in charge, to see to the butter lamps and incense; and the kitchen servants would also have to stay. During the day it was the custom for them at this time to dry pats of cow dung on the outside wall of the monastery; and they saw to it that the cats and any pet dogs that had been left behind got fed. At night they had to patrol through the many empty chapels all over the monastery, and as they did the rounds they beat a drum which would be handed over to the man who was going to do the next beat.

It would have been impossible for any lay official to keep order in Lhasa when it was so full of monks; so it had long been the custom for complete control of the city to be handed over during the Great Prayer to two Proctors, called Shengo. They were always chosen from Drepung and the right to the office was supposed to go to the senior monks in seccession, but if a monk whose turn it was did not think he could do the work properly, he could sell his right to another. As a rule it was a senior Dob-dob monk who secured the post and his body of attendants and officers were also Dob-dobs. It would have been difficult for anyone else to keep the crowds of monks quiet. The Shengo were usually strong, powerful men and they made themselves look broader by padding their shoulders, and taller by wearing boots with thick, high soles. They looked very impressive in wide red cloaks and brocade waistcoats and high yellow crest - like hats. Their attendants were the biggest and toughest monks they could find. They too wore heavily padded, voluminous clothes and had bright red strips of silk, sometimes tied in a resary, round their brawny bare right arms. The two chief attendants carried long, stout, silver rods in front of the Shengo as their mark of office; another senior attendant had an enormous, heavy wooden pole which was supposed to be for measuring the monks tea in the huge cauldrons in which it was made outside the Cathedral during the ceremony; the other attendants carried long willow branches, or thin wooden poles to keep order in the crowds.

Being a Shengo was a profitable business for they had wide powers to impose taxes and fines of various sorts and also to grant special licenses and privileges. At this time the streets of Lhasa were unusually clean because householders had to pay a fine if any dirt was seen in front of their houses; white lines were drawn across corners and alley ways where people used to relieve themselves and if anyone was caught doing so they were beaten and fined. Women were not allowed to wear ornaments unless they paid for the privilege. Even the great ladies were not exempt, but they stayed indoors as much as possible. One year there was a big fuss because the Shengo tried to make all women pay to wear the striped apron which is a part of their traditional daily dress. That was going too far, and the order had to be withdrawn. Anyone who put bells on a horse or mule or even a lap dog had to pay. There were all sorts of ways of extorting money and the Shengo were often quite cruel in doing so, but only a Dalai Lama could do anything to stop them. In fact they used to boast that there were only two people higher than themselves -- the Dalai Lama and the Chief Abbot of Ganden.

It certainly was necessary to have strict discipline during the Great Prayer. Drepung and Sera had long standing feuds and rivalries that could easily have led to trouble, but everyone was afraid of the Shengo who would flog mercilessly anyone caught fighting. We from Sera always thought that since the Shengo were from Drepung they would favour their own monks, so we tried to keep well out of their way. In fact, they were just as hard on monks of Drepung as on anyone else if they found them doing anything wrong.

The reason for this great gathering of monks was to hold communal prayer services for the good of all living creatures almost continuously for eighteen days. There were three assemblies in the Cathedral every day, one at about 5 to 7 in the morning, the next from 11 to 2 and the third from 4 to 6 in the evening. We all recited the prayers. Special rituals were performed and sermons preached by the Abbots, including the Tri Rimpoche, the Chief Abbot of Ganden, who was always the most learned monk and most skilful in debating in all Tibet. On one day the Dalai Lama himself used to preach a sermon sitting on a throne in the open, outside the Cathedral so that everyone could see and hear him. But the greatest interest for the ordinary monks was the frequent distribution of food and presents of money. There were many endowments to provide for such distributions and it was a great occasion for rich and pious laymen to undertake the principal expenses of the ceremony, particularly if they were allowed to invite the Dalai Lama to the Cathedral at that time. Any noble who was given the privilege tried to do better than any of his fellow noblemen; so huge sums of money were spent. The quality of the food and the size of the cash present differed on different days, and when it was known that they would be comparatively poor, fewer monks would attend. However there was always a big crowd. The Shengo and their attendants saw to it that we behaved properly and sat, wrapped in our big cloaks, with our heads held down respectfully. We were not even allowed to make smacking noises with our lips when we ate during the assemblies, and when the distribution of money took place outside we had to line up quietly.

We were supposed to give the alms we got to our teacher, and everyone did give them something; but no one gave them the whole lot, and there were ways of getting more than one's proper share. As there was such a crush of monks lining up to receive the hand - out, some managed to get a double share by holding out two hands, one on each side of the person in front, or they might join the line more than once. If the officials in charge recognized the monk, they might let him get away with it if they knew him and thought they might get a share - otherwise they would tell the servants to give him a beating.

On the 15th day of the month huge leather - covered frames decorated with all sorts of designs, figures, images and scenes, were put up round the central square in the middle of which the Cathedral stood. Some of the frames must have been about 60 feet high, and various monasteries and colleges took immense trouble making them and modelling the decorations and pictures which were all of coloured butter. There were beautiful religious scenes, deities, flowers, sacred emblems and so on, all in bright colours; others had clever tricks on them and one that was very popular was the figure of an oracle priest that raised its arms and wagged its head.

The display was not ready until after dark when it was lit up by lamps and torches. It was specially for the lay people and as they had been rather careful to keep out of the way so long as the monks dominated the city, they came pouring into the streets and surged round the square in groups singing and laughing, and often a bit drunk. Many of the noble families took Dob-dob monks with them as bodyguards, but all other monks were forbidden to go into the streets until dawn. However, some of us used to put on lay dress and join the crowds. It was a cheerful, noisy occasion with perhaps a little fighting now and then. As soon as the sun was up the frames were dismantled and the great mass of butter was sold, usually to leather workers who used it for dressing hides.

Although the Great Prayer assemblies actually went on for another week, the solemnity and tension of the ceremony were really broken by the fun of the 15th evening. A short verse says just that "the tight cord of the Great Prayer is cut by the butter - offerings of the 15th day". After that, too, the daily distribution of presents became smaller and a great many monks went back to their monasteries. As well as having had many good meals, we might be richer by as much as, say, £30.

Even when the monks who had stayed on left Lhasa on the 21st day, the celebration of the New Year was far from being over, but it then became mainly the business of the laymen. There were parades and processions of horsemen wearing ancient armour. One day there was a ceremony when the Coming Buddha was invited to hasten his arrival, and an image of him was pulled round the Cathedral on a wooden cart. There were sports in his honour, wrestling, carrying a heavy stone, and races by men on foot and by riderless horses.

Almost every month of the year has some important ceremony and although everything was done in a rather depressed mood that year because the Dalai Lama was still absent on the Indian frontier, and no one knew what the Chinese would do next, no one could ever think of doing without them, least of all the Great Prayer.

VII
BECOMING A DOB - DOB - FIGHTING MONK

One reason why I was called back from Dagpo was that the Labrang had been asked to provide the college with a novice to learn to play musical instruments for the religious services. I was told to join the class who were to learn the *gyaling,* which is a sort of aboe with a wide brass and copper mouth. It was quite strenuous work and meant a lot of practising. The lessons began in the spring and our teacher was a one - armed monk who had lost the other in a fight. He was a Dob dob. I have mentioned them several times and will soon explain about them. Fortunately he was kind, unlike some other teachers who have all sorts of harsh and cruel tricks and seem to think that pupils will learn quicker if they are lashed regularly on the arms and legs. But our teacher was not like that. It was not particularly difficult to learn the fingering. We were taught little rhymes to make us get the rhythm right; "soup is boiling, soup is boiling" or "long - legged teacher, long - legged teacher"; another tune was supposed to sound like a horse neighing. We had to learn to follow a score which was written on a large banner in a continuous line, not in separate notes; and the teacher conducted by following the line with his finger.

The difficult part was learning to blow continuously. This seems to surprise people in Europe who play wind instruments; but we had to go on blowing for hours without stopping to take breath. It is all a matter of breathing through the nose but it takes time to get right. One lesson was to blow through a reed into a saucer of water and keep a dry patch clear the whole time. For two months we had to practise all day, blowing non - stop for two hours at a time before we could rest. We sat in a grove of poplar trees outside the monastery and were not allowed shelter of any other sort. A whole lot of us would be sitting there blowing away either on oboes or on the long copper horns which produce a deep booming note. It certainly mode a splendid noise, but it was tiring work and we needed a lot of good food to be able to stand the strain.

At the end of two months we were examined by senior members of the whole monastery. That was an ordeal because it was the custom for them to make the test as difficult as possible. The player is expected to hold his gyaling exactly level with his shoulders the whole time; and the examiners held bunches of nettles under our naked armpits to make sure we kept our arms up. Worse, they hung a bag of sand on the end of the instrument because they said we had to be able to hold up properly even the heaviest ceremonial gyalings, which are ornamented with gold. At all events, I passed. But after all that hard work I only played once at a big ceremony. All the same I enjoyed having learnt to play, and I still like playing the Tibetan flute. I also enjoy hearing western music for the flute, oboe or clarinet and I am sorry I can't play a western - style oboe properly because my fingers are too short. Bach and Mozart are my favourites, and I have several tape recordings. Of course, I had no idea of that sort of music when I was in Tibet. Apart from our own music, all I heard in Lhasa were Chinese and Indian songs on gramophones or wireless in some of the shops.

Dote Chandzo, who came back to Labrang not long after me, gave me another task as well. I was sent to the house of a noble family to learn from their cook, who had been trained in western cooking in India. The family was that of Taring. The Taring Minister and his Lady are now in India where they work very hard looking after Tibetan refugee children in Homes and Schools in Mussoorie. I learnt quite quickly in their kitchen and didn't stay very long.

In spite of the new jobs I had to learn I did not feel really useful or contented and I was still as strongly attracted as ever to the company of the monks I have mentioned, called *Dob - dob*. Now, at last, I was old enough to join them. No one can be enrolled as a fully - fledged Dob - dob until he is mature and well - grown but I was now big and strong enough to be considered as a candidate. I spoke to my uncle about it, but he was not at all in favour and told me I would be much more sensible to try to get myself a teacher. He was quite calm about it and didn't really scold me when I said I was determined to go my own way. And so, with the help of my friend Sonam who had already been taken on as a candidate, I got myself accepted in the association of Dob - dobs to which he belonged.

The Dob - dob are a special body of monks, found only in the great monasteries of Drepung, Sera and Ganden, distinguished for their physical strength and courage. Young monks who are strong and active and who can't find a teacher or are bad at learning, are drawn to join one of the groups into which the Dob - dob organize themselves and which go in for the most strenuous sports and exercises. They used to meet, as soon as it was light, in a sandy valley to the west of Sera, take a shower under a cold waterfall or a dip in a little stream and then run naked in the sand, wrestle, or practise carrying and throwing heavy stones. The most important exercise was long - jumping off a raised ramp and formerly there were great competitions with the Dob - dob of Drepung who were Sera's long - standing rivals. The competition had to be stopped some time ago because there was a big fight and a monk was killed; but it was a Dob - dob's ambition to be a good jumper and tough and skilful in all sports.

They did not study books, at least when young, though some of them took trouble to learn to read and write. But they did learn some prayers by heart. One of their tasks was to play the oboe and long trumpet at ceremonies. I think Dote Chandzo sent me to learn music because he knew I wanted to be a Dob - dob. He was one himself and had been involved in a famous fight with a Dob - dob of Drepung, whose teeth he knocked out with a pestle. Dob - dobs could be recognized by the special way they wore their monk's dress. The skirt part of it was longer than usual, but they kept it kilted up rather higher than the ordinary monks. That gave them a bulky look round the thighs which they exaggerated by swinging their buttocks as they walked. Their hair was worn rather long, with a big curl trained round the left ear and down on to the cheek, and they often blackened their faces round the eyes to make themselves look fierce. Round their bare right arm, just above the elbow, they always tied a red silk scarf, and they usually had a big, heavy key hanging from their girdle not so much for use as for a weapon.

Dob - dobs are an accepted institution and are recorded as such in the books of their khamtsen. They are not supposed to wear their long locks in the monastery, especially inside the assemby hall; but they manage to hide them by tucking them behind their ears. However, those who are chosen as assistants to the Shengo at the Great Prayer can't get away with that, and have to sacrifice their treasured hair. To make up for it, they paint a lock in black soot on their cheek and keep it there until the real thing has grown again. Dob - dobs have all sorts of jobs to do as well as playing musical instruments and being a sort of monastery police. They go as bodyguards to monastic officials on their travels;they may even hire themselves to lay officials as travelling escorts. Many of the younger ones help to make and serve the tea in the various assemblies. Those who are good at business or understand farming may become stewards or treasurers of a Labrang, like Dote Chandzo, or of the country estates of a khamtsen.

I know that they have been given a bad name in western books, as quarrelsome, violent bullies who terrorized other monks and went in for immoral practices. That is by no means the whole truth. Any Tibetan will tell you that they are not only often amazingly strong and brave, but are also famous among all for open - handed generosity. It is true that they often fight, but what else can be expected if they are allowed to cultivate strength and daring? And it is true that their fights were often about favourite boys, but what else can be expected in a community of only men and boys? That sort of behaviour was not looked on as exceptionally bad, and probably the people of Lhasa preferred that monks should keep to themselves and not worry their womenfolk. Many of their fights and favourites were in a way just part of a game. It was a long - standing challenge to the Dob - dob to try to carry off some boy of a good family from Lhasa; and that led to fights in the city.In the monastery, too, some of them felt they had to have a fight now and then to prove they were strong and afraid of nothing. There was often no question even of a quarrel, but one of them would challenge some other Dob - dob who fancied himself as a fighter. But it is not true that they spent all their lives in fighting and indulgence. Many never fought at all; and many lived together in lifelong friendship of a simple and natural kind. The toughest of them were often the most generous, and would give away their money freely to some poor monk who was in difficulties, and to laymen too.

The association I joined had about 36 members who came from different colleges all over the monastery. That made it possible to meet a lot of new friends. There was no entrance fee, but each member contributed what he could to a common fund from which we bought food, which we ate in one another's rooms. Usually meetings were held in the room of the leader who was that one - armed monk who had taught me the oboe. He had been a famous jumper and fighter, but was very quiet in his manner though he saw to it that discipline was properly kept. Clubs of that sort, which we called *kyidu* -- that means that everyone shares the good and bad alike -- might last for many years or might break up and reform into new groups. If a member died, a share of his property went to the kyidu, some went to pay the men whose duty it was to cut up his dead body, and the rest to his college.

When I joined the Dob - dob I went to live with my friend Sonam, who had a room of his own. It was a pleasant change from the kitchen of the Labrang which was always full of people. After a few months I took leave and went home to Tshapanang to help with the harvest. Monks who were not bookmen were allowed to do so if they got permission from their college. Bookmen could not easily get leave of absence for more than a few days, and if they stayed away too long, they would be fined. At home, I wore lay dress but was always treated as a monk. Now that I was growing up I slept in the chapel room and looked after the butter lamps and incense. It was quite usual for monks who could be spared from the monasteries to go home and help on the land. Others used to go out and work on other peoples' land for hire, and some years a number of Dob-dob from Sera came to help my father with the harvest. They stayed in the chapel room and were well fed by our family and were always well - behaved and would recite prayers in the evening. Their pay was given in grain, and they usually received a present of butter as well. The only work a monk would not do was to plough, as that is forbidden by our religious rules.

Father was too busy with the business of hiring his animals to take much part in the harvesting but, even when he did not get monks to come, it was never difficult to find labour to help the family. At the end of the harvest there was a farmers' ceremony, when a Bonpo priest in a white robe came along and performed some ritual at the white stone that was kept in the middle of each field as an offering to the spirits of the soil. A little part of the crop was always left standing round it, and at the end of the harvest a sheaf was collected from each of the fields and made up to look like a figure. A man got inside it and carried it into the house singing "I stayed outside in the gales all winter and in the rain all summer, in the middle of your fields. Now take me into the house and I shall be happy and give you good crops". Then the sheaves are put on top of the grain store and left there until sowing time next year when they were taken out to the fields and put near the white stone.

Of course, we had a party, too. Some contributions to it were made from money or flour collected at other times of the year. For instance, at weeding time the man or woman who finished last had to pay a small fine; and when the crops had sprouted the women would take handfuls of green shoots and offer them to people riding past. There was a little song they sang asking the traveller to take the summer shoots and enjoy good luck. In return the traveller gave them a small tip.

That year I had a bad fall from one of the horses. My brother Dorje and I had taken the donkeys and horses down to the river to wash the dust and chaff off them after they had finished the job of carrying the crop from the fields to the threshing ground near the house. Father had a favourite stallion which was very strong and rather wild. It was sometimes given scorpions to eat after the stings had been taken out and sometimes a lizard. Those things are supposed to give great strength and be good for a horse's coat. When we were ready to go back from the river I wanted to ride the stallion. Dorje told me not to, but I got onto a tussock and managed to catch its mane and jump on its back. The stallion didn't like that at all and bolted for home, kicking about as he went. I was stark naked and had great difficulty in staying on and of course I couldn't control him as there were no reins. We dashed helter - skelter across the fields for the stable door. There was no chance of clearing the low gateway so when I saw that coming I fell off just in time. I was knocked unconscious for a time, and got some bad bruises and scratches. Father was rather angry with me for being so foolish.

Dorje was rather a strange fellow, and not very clever. He kept to himself and spent most of his time looking after the sheep belonging to the Che college of Sera which had property round Tshapanang. He got two lambs a year as a reward and it was quite a good job, but not so free and easy as life in the drokpas' country because there was always a steward from the monastery living in the village and keeping an eye on the workers. Dorje, also, made some money out of fishing in the river. That is something which is usually forbidden to people in Tibet, but there was a special custom that the villagers of Tshapanang and another village on the other side of the river might catch fish. My father did not like it because there is a religious objection to killing fish, so Dorje used to sell his catch secretly, or sometimes in the autumn he made soup of the fish and fed it to the dzo. I never ate fish in Tibet, and in winter, especially at the time of the Great Prayer, we were not supposed even to mention the word "fish". If we had to talk of them they must be called "water radishes".

About this time Dorje had an adventure that made him quite well known in the neighbourhood. One day when he was on the hills with his sheep, a leopard killed one of them. He heard the noise and ran there to find the leopard tearing at the sheep in a small ravine. He jumped on top of it and tried to throttle it; but it was terribly strong and fierce and he could not kill it. It bit and scratched and tore at him, but somehow he managed to lift it up and got it over his back, and carried it all the way down to the village still scratching and tearing and snarling. Everyone was astonished and terrified, but another man succeeded in stabbing it to death. Dorje was in terrible state. He lost one eye; his face was all torn and twisted and his back was terribly wounded. But he survived, though his face was a horrible sight, and he could never speak properly again. He got a lot of praise from everyone and the steward of the monastery gave him a big reward. Then he took the leopard's body round the neighbouring villages to show it to people there who all gave him presents. They were amazed that he should tackle a leopard with his bare hands. It was certainly brave but very rash.

VIII
MY FIRST FIGHT

When I was at home I told my father that I wanted to leave the Labrang for good. He never failed to help me, so when the time came for me to go back he came with me to make the arrangements. Dote Chandzo did not particularly like it, but he was quite patient as always. It is not unusual for a monk to go somewhere else if he chooses. The late Lama had really been my teacher and although Dote Chandzo had formally taken charge of me when the Lama died, that was not the same thing, and there was nothing to prevent me leaving. In fact, Dote was very generous and gave me furniture, carpets, copper pots, painted banners and some grain. It was the custom that, if a pupil left, the teacher would give him various presents for working for him. The pupil was supposed to give the teacher, who was responsible for feeding and clothing him, all the offerings he received in the monastery assembly; but Dote Chandzo had never expected me to give him anything so he was really more generous than he needed to be.

Now I was recorded as a novice monk of Kongbo Khamtsen, no longer as belonging to Sharpa Labrang, and I went back to stay with Sonam. As Dob - dob candidates we had to work for the *kyidu* for several months, cooking for the others and cleaning their rooms and doing odd jobs. We used to go to their exercises every day but were not allowed to take part in the jumping until we were full members. We were under the orders of the jumping master, who kept very strict discipline. We had to lay out our clothes tidily in the right order and only run or throw stones where and when we were told. The master controlled the jumping practice of the Dob - dobs and carried a spade handle with which he marked the distances. It was used, too, to keep order if the candidates were noisy or played the fool. The whole business was taken very seriously. My work in the khamtsen was to look after the horses but there were a lot of novices there, so I did not have nearly so much to do as in the Labrang.

Some days Sonam and I went to the morning assembly in our college and then, when I had finished my work, we would go about with our friends in the *Kyidu*. Through one of them, called Dawa, I met an older Dob - dob from Drepung known as Nechung Batsa -- "Pockmarked Nechung" -- because his face was deeply pitted with smallpox scars. Although there was a traditional rivalry that did not prevent us making friends with monks in Drepung. We often met them in Lhasa and sometimes went quite easily to their colleges. And on our special ceremony in Sera, when a very holy dagger with three sides which fell from heaven was brought out to be displayed, the monks of Drepung were always invited to be present. They wore their yellow hats on their left shoulder so as to be recognized, and we entertained them to lunch.

We always thought we were better off at Sera than the Drepung monks because when supplies were distributed every year they only got grain, but we got flour. There was a saying "If he has grain in his pocket, he's from Drepung: if he has flour on his ear, he's from Sera". That flour distribution was quite an occasion. It was done by lay servants who were astonishingly quick at ladling out the right amount to each comer. They had to practise for weeks ahead, using sand; all the same, at the distribution flour was flying everywhere, and the servants were white from head to foot at the end of it.

It probably sounds as though we Dob - dobs did not live a very religious life; but I never forgot that I was a monk. One day I had a most auspicious vision. I was walking along the hillside behind Sera when I saw what I thought was a great bull looking at me through some rocks. I could only see its head and neck, which were a glowing red colour, like blood, with bright shining horns. I ran back and called some friends who came to look; but we found nothing. They said I must have seen Jigche, the greatest of the protector deities, and that I was very lucky. Another day, about the same time, I saw a black dog carrying a man's head in its mouth. Sonam said I should have tried to get hold of it, as it had magical powers and would have made me very rich.

There was a much stranger experience that a great many people in our college shared. An elderly monk had died and the funeral rites had been held. His body had been lying in his room for three days, all tied up ready to be taken to the place where it would be cut in pieces and given to the dogs and vultures, when suddenly some monks who were standing in the courtyard saw him staggering down among them. He was naked and his body was a dull greyish colour. He must have broken the bands which tied him up. There was a great shout of alarm and cries of "Rolang, Rolang!" "A walking corpse, a walking corpse!". I ran to see what the noise was about. By then the dead monk had fallen to the ground and a brave Dob - dob was knocking his head with a stone. We believe that it sometimes happens that an evil spirit takes possession of a dead body, and can do great harm unless it is controlled. Some specially powerful mystics can dominate such evil spirits and make them work for them; but to most people an apparition of that sort is ·very dangerous. A special ceremony was held and the body was eventually cut up. Several of us went along to see in case anything strange should happen, but fortunately there were no bad effects.

The men whose duty it is to cut up the bodies of the dead do this on a huge flat boulder at a corner of a hill near Sera. When they are at work the dogs and vultures all come crowding round to be fed. The vultures are so tame that they come right up to the men when they are called. I sometimes went to get a few vulture feathers which mulemen like for making ornaments for their mules.

In the summer of that year, the Dalai Lama came back to Lhasa and I went with the rest of the Sera monks to the summer palace of Norbulingka to do homage and get his blessing. Then Chinese soldiers began to arrive. The first batch came on camels and looked shabby and ill - fed; they did not seem to have many weapons and the Lhasa people did not think very much of them at first. The Chinese tried to make friends and offered silver dollars in payment for whatever they bought. They seemed easy game for the Lhasa pickpockets who got away with a lot of their fountain pens and so on. But soon tents began to appear all over the place and more and more Chinese troops were to be seen. They had large numbers of mules and camels and some had jeeps and motor cycles. Before long they were beginning to take over people's houses. They offered a good price but it was made quite clear there was little choice but to accept. They behaved as if they owned the place; and ordinary people were afraid that when the Chinese got possession of some of the large houses a great many of those who were living there as shopkeepers, tenants and hangers - on would be turned out and find it difficult to live. Prices went up quickly and everyone became discontented. Our government tried to persuade the Chinese to take away some of their troops who were eating up all the supplies.

Then the Chinese forced them to dismiss the two leading ministers who had spoken up for the people. That made us all angry and worried.

About that time I was, I suppose, nearly 15 and, as a Dob - dob candidate, I was on the look - out for a chance to prove my strength and spirit to my friends. In fact, I was quite ready for a fight if one offered. And I had my first that winter before the New Year.

I was waiting one morning on the stone steps outside the Assembly Hall with a lot of other monks. There had been a little snow and we were standing about, wrapped up in our cloaks, trying to warm up in the sun before the gates were opened. I was on the edge of the stone balustrade of the stairway when another monk pushed me off. He was a boy I knew slightly and disliked. There was no particular reason; we just did not like one another; you know how it is. He laughed when I stumbled into the snow, and that made me furious. I leaped at him and hit him on the head with my wooden tea bowl -- we all carried them in the pouch of our robe. Other monks restrained us because we had to go into the Assembly, where we glared at one another from a distance. I got out first and lay in wait for him and threw several stones at him. He rushed at me swinging his big key on a strap and hit me on the head. He nearly knocked me out and I was streaming with blood but I had a knife and managed to get at him and hit him in the side and knocked him down. Then I made off in a hurry. Of course, I ought not to have been carrying a knife. That is strictly forbidden except for the monks of a special monastery who carry one with a long flexible blade for making dough offerings. But most Dob - dobs usually had a knife about them somewhere, and sometimes in a fight a monk might get killed. If that happened the killer would be terribly beaten and thrown out of the monastery in a dirty white garment. And anyone found carrying a knife would be flogged even if he had never used it. So I was a bit anxious until I heard that the other boy was not badly hurt.

Lots of people had seen the fight so the Proctors soon heard about it and sent their servants to bring us to them in the Assembly Hall. They asked briefly what had happened and we told the truth. They immediately ordered us to be flogged. The other boy was beaten first and he got 30 double strokes because he had started the fight. I had to kneel on my bare knees and watch. Then the four servants caught hold of me and laid me face downwards on the floor; my robe was pulled up and I was flogged with willow branches by two servants, one on each side, who gave me 25 strokes each in quick succession. Fortunately I knew the servants and they did not take too long about it. It was very painful and drew blood, but I didn't cry out. It would have been the end of me as a Dob - dob if I had. I bit the fold of my cloak between my teeth to help me.

The other boy and I made it up after that; at least, we did not fight again though we didn't really like each other any better. My Dob - dob friends were quite pleased with me; and I was quite pleased with myself, too. My buttocks and legs were bruised and sore for a long time but Sonam spread raw egg on them and I lay face downwards in the sun whenever I could. Plentiful dressings of butter helped, too; but I suffered a good deal for about a month. I have the marks still.

Sonam and I went to the Great Prayer again that year, and stayed in the Shasur house, which was better than the Oracle's chapel. I was particularly careful to keep out of trouble with the Proctors.

Not long after the New Year my Drepung friend, Nechung Batsa, asked me if I would like a new job. He had a great reputation for fearlessness; and he and Dawa sometimes acted as bodyguard to a monk official at Lhasa who was their patron. The official, Tsetrung Lobzang Yonten -- Tsetrung means monk official and Lobzang Yonten was his name -- was appointed Governor of Kyirong, a district on the north - east border of Nepal and had asked Nechung Batsa and Dawa to go with him. He told them to find another helper as well, and they suggested that I should join them. I was delighted at the prospect, because I had heard that Kyirong was a pleasant place and I liked the idea of getting away from the monastery again.

I went with my friends to see the Governor, who accepted me and promised us all good pay. He said we would have to help with the supervision of the farmers and the collection of taxes. It might be thought I was rather too young for such work, but I had gained experience among the herdsmen and I was strong and self - confident. So once more I changed from monk's robes into lay dress - a cloak, tunic and trousers of dark red homespun of good quality. The Governor provided me with a sword, which I wore proudly at my waist. I still kept my hair short because as a candidate I was not yet allowed to grow a long side lock, but I was allowed to wear the Dob-dob's red scarf on my right arm. Sonam and other friends were quite envious of my good luck in going to Kyirong, and I waited in excitement until we were ready to go.

IX
WITH A CORRUPT GOVERNOR IN KYIRONG

We were quite a fine cavalcade when we set out for Kyirong. The Governor mounted us on his own horses, and there were several servants and a lot of baggage animals. Kyirong was an important post, so the Governor had to make an impressive show on the road. He was entitled to free transport, shelter, and fodder at the villages along the way and I saw almost at once that my new master was a difficult person. He bullied the villagers and demanded all sorts of things he had no right to. I knew something about that kind of trouble from my father's experience in providing free transport to officials as part of his taxation. Sometimes the travellers were too exacting; but this Governor was exceptionally bad. He would never dream of giving a tip or any sort of present to the villagers who had to come in and work for him, and was much more likely to scold and shout at them. But Dawa and I used to give them tea and food without the Governor's knowledge.

Our journey took us through my home at Tshapanang, on to the Brahmaputra which we crossed in a wooden ferry boat, over a high pass leading to the great Yamdrok lake, and from there to Tashilhunpo. It was about May and travelling was very pleasant; the water of the lake was deep blue and there were fresh green willows in the villages.

I remember that when we were coming in to Tashilhunpo I was riding ahead and we had to cross quite a big river that flows down from Gyantse. There is a stone bridge, but for some reason the Governor told me to look for a crossing place. I was still rather an inexperienced traveller and instead of looking for fast rippling water I chose a track leading down to a stretch of calm blue water into which I rode my horse. We plunged in deep, right over the horses back. I got soaked and everyone laughed; but it didn't matter and I soon dried off.

Tashilhunpo, where we stayed for some days, is another great and very beautiful monastery like Drepung and Sera. There is a row of tall buildings topped with gilded roofs , which are the tombs of the past Panchen Lamas. Discipline there seemed to be very strict and the Dob - dob, of whom there were very few, did not seem to have nearly so much freedom as we had. They said they had to get permission to go to the town of Shigatse nearby, and when they came back in the evening they had to pass two proctors at the monastery gate, who sniffed at their breath to see whether they had been drinking. Most of them had been to beer shops, and they said they used to trick the proctors by inhaling rather than breathing out.

After Tashilhunpo we stayed in another great monastery, Sakya, which is the oldest in that part of Tibet. It was rather a frightening place with huge dark, dusty buildings and not many monks about. Its Lamas are famous for their magical powers and control a great number of witches and famale spirits through which they send messages all over Tibet. I was told that the six most powerful are tied to a straw pillar in one of the halls; they appear to have human bodies and their heads are covered with fleas. One day in the week they take possession of six monks, who perform a dance carrying red - hot vases on the palm of their hands. At the end, they put some goat fat on a fire and that seems to make any women who are watching go into hysterics. When I saw it, a party of drokpa women pilgrims ran away in terror. In the evening for about three hours no one goes out because of the danger from magic ceremonies that are being performed. When they are over, a thigh - bone trumpet is blown. My friends told me to be very careful there not to talk to any pretty girl or even to pick up a coloured thread that you might see on the road; and if you borrowed someone's cloak or blanket you should take good care to spit on it before using it, otherwise you might fall into the power of a witch.

Even in Lhasa people were afraid of those witches, and when I was living there later I sometimes heard a cry going round "A Sakya witch is out!". Then everyone would hurry indoors, or, if they had to be outside, they would carefully avoid speaking to any strange women they might see. People who did come under a witch's influence behaved in all sorts of strange ways, and if it was not certain whether someone was genuinely possessed or not, the test was to put a hot iron on his hand. If he was possessed, the iron would leave no mark and the man, when asked, would name the witch or spirit that was troubling him. Then if it was a witch and if you could trace her, you would find the mark of the iron on her hand.

One famous Sakya witch lived at Lhasa. She had married a rich Ladakhi trader and kept a cloth shop. She was short and stout and had a very red face and a large black mole under one eye. If a man has a mole like that, it is very auspicious and means he is likely to get great power or wealth; but in a woman it is a bad and dangerous sign. People said that the woman paid taxes to Sakya for permission not to go back there and be kept under the Lama's control; but, whatever was the truth, everyone went out of their way not to offend her.

It was about a month before we reached Kyirong, where the Governor took over from his monk predecessor. He also met his lay colleague, for in every big district there are usually two governors, one a monk and one a layman. The Dzong, or District Headquarters, was a fine big building like a fortress, with plenty of good rooms. All round there were trees and shrubs, green fields, flowers, many clear streams and hot springs, and we looked out on magnificent snow mountains on the frontier with Nepal. The valley of Kyirong is much lower than Lhasa and is very fertile with all kinds of crops, vegetables, and fruit including wonderful apples and peaches. There were rich pastures for cows and fine grazing for yaks on the higher slopes. It was a big village of about a hundred houses, and the people were friendly and good-looking. I dont think I have known a better place, before or since.

Part of my work was to go to the fields and see that the farmers sowed them properly and looked after them and, finally, to make sure we got our share of the crop, as tax, when it was harvested. As an assistant to the Governor I was now a person of some importance and was called Kusho, Sir, instead of being addressed as a mere novice. A very important job was to supervise the levy of a tax on the export of sheep to Nepal. The frontier was at a bridge about a day's journey from the village; there were Nepalese soldiers on the other side of the bridge. Every other month I had to go down there with a representative of the lay governor to do my turn of duty. We had a house and our own servants near the bridge and that was the customs post where we counted the sheep and took the money. Hundreds of sheep were driven down every year but it was forbidden to export ewes and we had to keep an eye on that. I tried to make things easy for the Tibetan traders and they often gave me small presents, especially if I let them take a ewe out as I did sometimes if I was convinced the owner needed the sale price to keep him alive. The Nepalese had their own customs post and a small party of soldiers on the far side of the bridge. We did not collect any taxes from Nepalese traders but we kept an account of the number of them who came into Tibet. They often gave us little presents too, usually cane sugar or matches, so it was quite a profitable job. On one of my visits to the frontier, a party of Chinese soldiers arrived. They examined the bridge and put up a notice there and then they went away.

At the end of my month of duty, Dawa or some other assistant came to take my place and I went back to work at the Dzong. I got on well with the villagers at Kyirong because I am a farmer and peasant myself by birth, and I knew from my father what a nuisance officials can be. The people were very willing to be friendly and I was welcome in their houses, which they kept beautifully clean. They were handsome and prosperous, and generous, too. There was a pleasant custom of hanging a basket full of potatoes cooked with garlic outside each house and anyone who liked could take one; or they might put out apples and peaches in season; and on a table inside the door was a pot of chili sauce to dip the potatoes in if you wanted. Their potatoes were delicious and there was plenty of rice, too, which came from Nepal, and excellent barley beer. Parties seemed to be always going on. The two Governors gave them sometimes, and sometimes the Nepalese officer who lived in Kyirong, or the Governor of the Dzongka District which lay to the north of us. If we went there it was a long day's journey, so we would spend a day or two enjoying ourselves before going home.

It should have been a very happy time in that beautiful and friendly place but unfortunately our master turned out to be a bad - tempered, extortionate bully. He drank a lot and was forever smoking either expensive cigarettes or Nepalese cheroots. And he was loose - living, too. We learnt that he had a mistress in Lhasa and he soon took another in Kyirong where the girls are famous for their beauty. He kept pressing Dawa and me to take mistresses but I was young and regarded myself as strictly bound by my vows so I didn't do so. All the same he was always accusing me of going with girls. Dawa eventually took a girl, whom he married, and gave up being a monk.

The Governor really treated us no better than servants. Dawa was the cook and was always being scolded. I had to make his bed and clean his room, or wait with his clothes ready when he wanted to dress. Often he shouted for me to bring his cloak when he was still in bed with his mistress. Someone gave her a little monkey and he made me look after it and keep it warm inside my shirt; it was a nice little monkey but terribly dirty. But it was no use complaining to him. He was always angry and rude and abused me one day like anything for taking one of his cigarettes.

And that was not all. He was cruel to the peasants and to anyone he did not like. When he lost his temper he would beat the victims savagely with his own hands. One unfortunate monk was kept in prison and beaten almost every day for some small offence, because he was too poor to pay a fine. The Governor often flogged him himself. I have never seen a Tibetan official do that except him. His lay colleague was a mild person, but was quite unable to do anything to stop the governor. Eventually he made a report to Lhasa. Of course, the Governor became very unpopular almost immediately. He tried to make money in every possible way. There were many wild animals all round Kyirong, including leopards; and he made a business of trapping them for their skins which brought a good price -- at least he made other people do the work for him without paying them for it, saying all they wanted was to be rid of the leopards.

The way the leopards were trapped was like this. The trapper made a small house which was divided into two compartments by a wall with a hole in it. A goat was tethered on the far side of the hole and a heavy wooden beam balanced so that when the leopard went through the hole, the beam fell on its head. It was particularly wicked for a monk to be responsible for taking life and it seemed worse that he made money out of it. I suffered from his leopard trapping, too, when he bought a lot of little Nepalese ponies which he got cheaply because they had mange. He had me rub them with the leopard's fat, which smelt horribly. The treatment did not do the ponies much good. Two of them died; and I got terrible red spots all over me. I had nothing to treat them with except vaseline, and they lasted about a year and gave me a lot of trouble.

The people were always being put to all sorts of difficulty. The Governor demanded additional taxes to which he had no right; and because he did not like living in the Dzong, he made them build a new house for him at the expense of the village. He really was a very nasty character. And he didn't even give us the pay he had promised. Nechung Batsa very quickly became fed up with him and left after only a few weeks. And Dawa left, too, not long after he got married. But I stayed on, hoping he would eventually pay me. In fact, I stayed in Kyirong for more than two years. The Governor kept on promising he would pay but he never did; and at last I lost my patience and told him I was leaving. He shouted furiously at me. As he still paid me nothing, I took several valuable things belonging to him, a good horse, a fine knife and other things. I told him I had done so and that I would leave at once. He was black with rage but did not dare to do anything because he knew that I could have reported to the monastery and the government about him.

So I went off by myself. On the way back I passed Tashilhunpo again but this time it was a sad sight because there had been a terrible flood in which many people of Gyantse, and further downstream, had been drowned. When I got near home I sold the horse for two donkeys and a bullock which I meant to leave with my father. I felt very happy at being on my way back; but it turned out to be a sad homecoming for I found that my mother had died. They had not been able to send word to me in Kyirong. My father was grieving greatly and I missed my mother very badly. She had been particularly fond of me and although my becoming a monk had separated us so early, there was always a special bond between us.

Before she died my mother had left instructions that I was to have her two fields which she had been given by the monastery. I discussed with my father what to do about them. I could have sold them to him or to someone else in the village. Or I could have arranged to have them in my own name and get them cultivated by him or by hired labour, in which case they would eventually have gone back to the monastery. We decided to have the fields recorded in my father's name and that he would give me a generous supply of barley and other necessities each year. Quite a lot of monks own land and other property such as sheep or yaks, and they may become quite rich because they do not have to pay much by way of taxation. But when they die most of their property goes to their college rather than to their family.

After spending a few days at home I went back to Sera where I again stayed with Sonam.

As for the Governor of Kyirong, the people could not endure him any longer so they got up a petition, which they sent to the government at Lhasa, saying they would all leave the village and go to Nepal unless he was removed. The headmen who took the petition to Lhasa were able to convince the government that they meant what they said; and as that would have been a big loss of revenue as well as a matter of shame. For such bad administration, an enquiry was held and the Governor was dismissed and punished. Of course, that cost the Kyirong villagers quite a lot, but it was a very good thing and it was bound to make future governors more careful.

When my former master came back to Lhasa I got Nechung Batsa to go with me to see him because I felt that I still had not had my dues for over two years work for him. He was just as angry and rude as ever and I got nothing more from him; but everyone could now see how mean and disreputable he was.

X
IN LHASA AND NYEMO

Things had changed a good deal by the time I got back to Lhasa. There were many more Chinese and a lot of new buildings put up by them. They were interfering in people's lives in various ways. Some of the things they introduced were useful such as horsedrawn carts with rubber tires; some had as many as four horses but only rich families could afford those. There were also light carts for one horse, and many bicycles which young people and shopkeepers found a help. A new hospital was quite popular. New schools were being opened, but opinion in the monasteries was suspicious about what was being taught there, because the Chinese were always telling us that everyone was equal and that religion was no use. They often gave film shows -- war films, farming, factories and so on -- but they were all meant to prove how clever and powerful the communists were; and people preferred the performances by conjurors and acrobats.

The biggest thing the Chinese were doing was making roads between China and Tibet, and also from Lhasa to Shigatse and other places. They used to pay Tibetan workers well for their labour but most of the work was done by Chinese prisoners who were treated very badly. The new roads brought a lot more motor traffic, including big lorries. We all disliked the noise and the smell very much. People in the villages through which they ran suffered from the roads, because there was less need for their donkeys and horses, and because the roads were too hard for the animals' feet. But people in distant villages who had wool to sell found them an advantage at first, for the Chinese sent men to buy the wool on the spot and carry it away in their lorries. Later on, when they had got a monopoly of the wool buying they fixed quite low prices and that did not please the flock owners so much.

We heard from a monk who had been in Kongbo that the Chinese were destroying the fine forests there for timber and firewood. They were also killing the bears, deer and other animals in large numbers.

In the places where they had cut down the forest they had grown potatoes, some as big as a man's head. They were very proud of these but the local people thought they were an evil omen.

By far the worst trouble was that the Chinese were gradually buying almost all the crops and the vegetables to feed their soldiers so that prices for the townspeople were always rising. The poor were particularly badly hit. There was a lot of complaining, too, because the Chinese had taken the Dalai Lama to Peking and nobody knew when he would come back.

All that did not worry me too much because I was now a fully - fledged Dob - dob and after so long a time away I enjoyed coming back to my *kyidu* and being allowed to take a more active part in all the activities. I was allowed to join the jumping exercises and had to train by running with my boots full of sand. As I had some money to spend I bought some good new clothes. Dob - dobs were always very proud of their clothes and looked after them carefully. We liked a specially dark shade of expensive, fine woollen cloth for our long skirt - like garment. It had to be folded carefully into a number of pleats, rather like a kilt and when were in our rooms we usually took it off and put it under a board and sat on it to press the pleats. The front part had to be quite flat, again like a kilt. And I could now grow my hair long. There were strict rules about the exact length and manner in which it had to be cut; the right side was brushed downwards and the left was bunched up into a big curl. We all took a lot of trouble to keep our hair well and rubbed it regularly with vaseline.

For a month or so after I got back from Kyirong I managed to avoid doing much work, but I did go round the college several times to make sure that the older monks were all right. That was regularly done by the Dob - dob, and if anyone was ill or needed help it was generally the Dob - dob who looked after them. Still, there was plenty of spare time, and a party of us used to go in to Lhasa most days. Some of the older Dob - dob would go to a restaurant, or a gambling house or go to look for girls; but I was not interested in those things and what I liked to do was to go where there was singing and dancing and where I could play the flute. We sometimes went to see a sort of gypsy people, called Lorogpa, who came into Lhasa in the autumn. They were very clever with horses and had all sorts of tricks to show them off to the best advantage in the horse market. You could always tell them because their cloaks were weighed down on one side, like a sack, by the mass of things they carried in them, such as fur bags for barley flour which they made from the skins of marmots, and metal teapot lids made from scrap metal they managed to collect or steal. Most people were suspicious of them, and disliked them for killing marmots. It really is distressing to see a màrmot cornered, because it holds up its paws as if it were praying for mercy, and it looks so pitiful. But those gypsies had a sort of connection with the monastery, because they came to buy the old tea leaves and discarded offerings made of flour and butter, so we came to know some of them quite well. We were never allowed, however, to buy their marmot skin bags because it is forbidden to use such things in a monastery, where we have to use cotton flour bags.

That winter I went again to the Great Prayer. There was a good deal of grumbling and discontent with the Chinese because they wanted to take away the authority of the Shengo to control Lhasa at that season. I stayed in Shasur's house; and got myself into another fight. I was going by myself early in the morning to reserve a place in the Cathedral when I ran into a party of big Dob - dob, from Drepung, who asked who I was. When I said I was from Sera they insulted me and tried to catch hold of me, saying they would carry me off to live with them. I threatened them with my key and broke away. A little later I found I was bleeding from a deep wound in my left thigh. One of them must have stuck a sharp knife into me, but I hadn't noticed it at the time. I thought they should not get away with that so I planned to look out for them and challenge them to a fight. I tried to get some of my friends to join me so that we could take on the lot of them. My friends advised me not to start a fight at the Great Prayer because the punishment, if I were caught, would be extra hard. All the same, I did meet one of the Drepung men later and hit him on the head with my key. He seized me by the throat, and we struggled while a lot of other monks looked on. An elderly monk from Sera separated us and, fortunately, we did not hear any more about it. Perhaps the Shengo were too worried about the Chinese to pay attention to a small scuffle like that, but we would have been in trouble if it had turned into a big fight.

Soon after the New Year a senior monk of Sera told me that one of his relations, who was treasurer to a noble family, was looking for someone to help him on their estate in Nyemo, which is some way west of Lhasa. Although I had not liked my master in Kyirong, I had enjoyed to work there and was quite ready for another job that would take me away from the monastery and give me some independence, provided I had a good master. I went to meet the treasurer, whom I found to be a kindly and humorous person, and as we took to one another he asked me to go with him when he left for Nyemo in the spring. His name was Kargye Chandzo, or rather that was a nickname, comparing him with the butter ornaments that are stuck on the spout and handle of a beer jug, because he had a broad face and big spreading ears.

Before it was time to leave Lhasa I went one day with Sonam to burn incense on a high hill overlooking Sera. It must have been the 15th day of the second month, because on the 15th of each month incense is burnt on several of the hills around Lhasa. The task is usually done in turn, month about, by the Dob - dob of Drepung and Sera, though sometimes kitchen servants may be sent instead. Incense is provided by the nobles and other rich patrons, who also give good presents of tea and money to those who are going to climb the hills. And very often the ordinary people, shoopkeepers and small traders, like to add a small handful of incense and give a small present. Serveral parties of at least two men go to the different hills. They start off overnight and on their way up they light fires at several places as a signal to the patrons that they are on their way. When they get to the top they rest in a sheltered place until dawn; then they set fire to a great pile of incense, chant a prayer, and throw a handful of flour in the air for good luck. People in the city always look out to see a great pillar of smoke rising from each of the hilltops. The air in the early morning is usually still and it is a lovely sight.

One of the places where incense has to be burnt is really very high and the party going there have to start a whole day before. It is not very popular because one year a monk was carried off by a Dzami, or "Rock - man", another sort of man - bear which you might call the Abominable Snowman. That kind throws stones very powerfully, but can only do so backwards between its legs. The hill Sonam and I climbed was not as high as that one but it was quite a stiff climb. We felt very happy when we saw our fire shooting up its thick white smoke and other fires answering it on the hills in all directions.

I was Kargye Chandzo's only assistant, so our party on the way to Nyemo was very simple compared with my journey to Kyirong, three years before. The road ran through country that was quite new to me, northwestwards up the Tolung valley about 8 miles from Lhasa, where the Chinese had made a new road to link up with an airfield on the upland plateau about 80 miles to the north. We travelled fast on the new road and then left it, turning to the west, and reached the great Karmapa monastery at Tsurpu. From there we crossed an easy pass up to a fine broad grazing ground with a view of miles and miles of snow mountains called Nyenchen Thangla. We camped there one night and it was like being back in the *drok*. From the high grazing plain we rode down into a wide oblong valley with good grass in it. That was part of Nyemo, but we had to go on, through a small gorge, to a lower valley where there were big houses and monasteries surrounded by fine willow and poplar trees. Before reaching Nyemo Dongkar, which was the name of the estate, we stopped and changed our clothes to make a good effect on arrival; then we rode smartly up to the estate house and were greeted by the steward and the farmers with scarves and tea.

The house was large and very old. It had nine stories and must once have been magnificent, but it was crumbling away now and the upper stories could not be used safely. Still, there were comfortable rooms and it looked out on to a beautiful grove of trees and a clear fast river. I had a good room to myself, and there were servants to look after me. An old monk lived in a small chapel over my room. I could hear him performing ceremonies at regular intervals, and his little skull - drum rattling and handbell ringing quite late at night and early in the morning. At one corner of the roof itself was a tiny shrine where a Bonpo priest in a white robe carried out his rituals for keeping away hail whenever there seemed a danger.

There were eleven people living in the house and working there and in the fields. Our headman used to get up about 5 every morning -- when the cock is putting his trousers on, as we say -- and call together the peasants for the day's work. I got up a bit later and had some tea or soup and then did my first job which was to hand out the tea and tsampa for the workers' rations. I gave them generous handfuls without trying to measure the exact quantity, for Kargye Chandzo was very sympathetic towards the villagers and did not want to be mean or sparing. He spent most of his time in the house and sent me to the fields to supervise the work there. The climate was mild but the soil was thin and stony there, and not very fertile; so the people were poor compared with those of Kyirong. In fact their crops had failed the year before, and the Government had had to give them barley to eat. Also they had had to borrow seed from the District Governor.

If I had wanted, I could have just sat about and watched them working but I liked to take a hand myself. I did not plough, of course, because monks may not do that; but I helped with the irrigation and weeding, and later at the harvest. The people were reserved at first, and not so easy going as in Kyirong and, like any villagers, they tried to get away with as much as they could; so I had a little trouble at the start. I was still quite small and young - looking, and some of them seemed to think they need not pay much attention to me. Within the first few days I saw some young men idling about, and one of them was ploughing very badly and carelessly. When I went up and stopped the plough cattle he shouted at me to get out of the way, so I hit him with a stick. He pulled me down and abused me saying I was no better than a girl and they didn't take orders from girls. I managed to get up and challenged him or any of his friends to a real fight, as any Dob - dob would do; but they didn't dare accept, so I got hold of a whip and hit the ploughboy while the others ran off. Later, when Kargye Chandzo heard what had happened he had some of them beaten by his servants. Not long after, I caught the son of one of the leading men trampling over the young barley with a donkey and a bullock. I was taking him to the Chandzo to make him pay the usual fine when his father came up and as he thought he was an important person he was angry and said I was just stirring up trouble. However, I took them both to the house where Kargye Chandzo had them beaten on the spot, not seriously but just to show them they must behave. After that, there was not much to worry about, though in the summer I did occasionally have to punish a few village children and even young men who used to crawl secretly into the fields of peas and beans which we grew for fodder. Lying flat on their backs to avoid being seen, they quietly picked as much as they could. If I caught any of them, they were fined or got a mild beating.

Another of my jobs was to collect payment due from the farmers for the willow branches which they cut for roofing their houses. There were plantations of pollarded willows all round the house and the profit from them went to repair the estate house itself.

When I knew the villagers better I came to like them, and I think they liked me too because I always tried to help them when they did their work properly. Kargye Chandzo was a particularly kind master, and knew all about their families   He never took bribes or asked for anything he was not entitled to; nor did I. In fact we had several meetings with the District Governor who lived at Mongkhar Dzong not far away, and we argued with him about the amount to be raised from Nyemo to pay the government dues. We managed to reduce that to the lowest possible sum, and the villagers were very grateful.

The Chandzo was very good company, always cheerful and generous. He gave me good food, clothes, and wages of five bushels of grain a month for which I could take the equivalent in tsampa, butter, and meat. He often gave me presents of money as well. I had servants, too, and a good horse whenever I needed one. Now and then there were parties with the stewards of neighbouring estates, and sometimes we went to a famous monastery which was quite near.

Harvest time was the most important and busiest season and I had to help the Chandzo to see that we got our proper share of the grain. I enjoyed watching the women harvesting the barley quickly and skilfully with their sickles, and then seeing it piled on the threshing floor and beaten with flails after the cattle had been driven round and round over it; then came the winnowing, the men using forks and the women holding up the grain in basket scoops and letting it trickle down while the breeze carried away the chaff. Autumn days in Nyemo were bright and warm, and work often went on late into the night. Each task had its special song, and it was beautiful to hear the singing while the moon lit up the threshing ground. When all was safely stored, the donkeys, which became covered in straw and dust when carrying the crops and the grain bags, were washed in the river, while the children splashed about and enjoyed the fun. At the end there were harvest celebrations and parties.

It was all very quiet and peaceful compared with Lhasa or Kyirong. We did not see anything of the Chinese or even hear much about them, though Kargye Chandzo, who sometimes got messages from Lhasa, was worried lest they should gradually find their way all over the country, and one or two things happened which seemed bad omens. We heard that a child with two heads had been born in another part of Nyemo, and later that a mule had given birth to a foal. The child and the foal both died, but that sort of thing was usually a sign of trouble. All the same, I would have been happy to stay in Nyemo for another year at least. But not long after the harvest I was called back to the khamtsen and told it was my turn to play the gyaling at the New Year ceremony in Sera, so I had to practise for that. When the time came I was lent specially smart clothes boots with high white soles and brocade uppers, a new yellow, crested hat, and a brocade water bottle cover to wear at my waist. That was, in fact, the only time I ever played at a ceremony; later when my turn came again, I paid another monk to take my place.

Some months after I had left Nyemo I heard that a party of Chinese had been there, giving talks about better farming and how the peasants ought to be equal with the landlords and no one should waste money on religious offerings.

XI
TEA-SHOP MANAGER IN LHASA

On the way back to Lhasa I had gone home for a short time. My father was still doing quite well though there were fewer traders than before who wanted to hire animals. The Chinese had taken a big share of the business and carried most of their goods in carts or jeeps. Otherwise they caused no great trouble in the villages and people did not see much of them except passing through or occasionally coming to give lectures. By now I thought I was old enough to have somewhere of my own to stay, so I asked my father if he would buy me a room in the khamtsen. He was always generous and he had saved up something for me from my mother's fields so he readily agreed. I went back to the khamtsen to look for a suitable room and I stayed with Tashi Tshering there until I could find one. He advised me to settle down quietly and try to learn; and he said I should cut off my long curl and attend the prayer assemblies. I am sure my uncle would have told me the same but he had been appointed as abbot of an important monastery north of Nepal where he became quite famous and rich.

It was not long before I was allowed to buy a room. It was quite small, with a tiny kitchen, and it looked out on to a narrow passage between two high buildings; but it was clean, and it was mine. Now I was able to put into it the furniture I had got from Doté Chandzo when I left the Labrang. My father gave me some carpets, and I had saved enough to buy other things I needed. That was the most pleasant time I had in Sera. I kept my room very clean. In fact, it was rare to find any monk who was slovenly in the way he kept his cell. There was a small altar of course, with images on it and with incense always burning or a small butter lamp. There were also the necessary offerings of pure water in small metal bowls. I had a basin to wash in, some Sunlight soap and a towel, and a bucket of water which the kitchen servants filled every day for a small tip. I felt very lucky to have a room of my own. Many poor monks spent most of their life in a sort of dormitory above the kitchen. There was no shame in that; and the clever ones usually managed to study hard and become learned and important monks, and so get their own rooms and pupils. Those who were not so successful were usually given a free room to themselves when they grew old. Some of them became rather eccentric. There was one in our college who spent all his time meditating by himself. He had no furniture in his room and seemed to be very poor; but people used to give him alms and he had gradually collected a large supply of silver coins which he washed and polished and put into bags which he hid in a hole behind the plaster on the wall of his cell. When he knew he was dying he drew a pigeon over the hole and wrote a verse saying "if the pigeon dies, open its breast". His death was not discovered for quite a long time. Then the college paid the expenses of his last rites and gave the room to another monk. Much later the new occupant thought there must be some meaning in the verse on the wall, so he dug behind the picture of the pigeon and found the money. Another old monk went about in terrible rags, but had a silver coin tied up in each strip of his robe. And there was another of a different sort who concentrated the whole time on reciting the special prayer to the goddess Drolma, which he did with such power that the goddess used to appear to him in his cell.

In spite of Tashi Tshering's good advice I wasn't ready to settle down yet. It was much more enjoyable to be a Dob-dob. My friends often came to meet in my room and we cooked whatever we had between us and had a good talk, or played dominoes, or sang. In winter there was a brazier of sheepdung on top of charcoal to keep us warm. After the last prayer assembly we were supposed to stay in our rooms by ourselves and the head of the khamtsen went round to see that all was quiet and that lights were out. We knew when he was coming and lay low; but after he had gone his rounds we would light the lamp again and stay there playing or talking until quite late. Then if it was cold we would all roll up in a ball under whatever blankets we had, and go to sleep. Or sometimes I went to my friends' rooms for the same sort of party; but we would be up in good time for our exercises in the morning.

Compared with the bookmen monks we Dob-dob were learning nothing. We did go to the assemblies when there was a good distribution of food or money; and we had to be careful to hide our curls which were not allowed to be worn there. Sometimes, too, we went to listen to the scholars practising debating in the poplar grove where this took place. We found this amusing and would imitate their gestures — stamping, waving, rosaries, clapping one hand against the other at arm's length, and uttering a shout when making a point. We may have picked up some of the argument, too; but the main reason for going was that there was a distribution of food and money there on some days.

Another thing that took us into the assemblies was that it was one of the Dob-dob's jobs to serve the tea. That was really work only for the young and strong. The metal teapots were very large and heavy and we had to run with them over floors slippery with the grease that the monks threw out of their bowls when they had drunk the tea. We scattered sand on it from time to time and once a year the floors were scraped and the grease was sold to people from east Tibet who used it for medicine or burnt it as incense in the houses of sick people. It smelt very nasty, but because it came from a monastery it was thought to be very powerful. There might be a good deal of roughness and jostling when the tea was being served, and if a Dob-dob could surprise in the kitchen passage someone he didn't like, he tried to bash into him with the heavy teapot or to pin him to the wall with it. The tea was made in the kitchens where the lay servants worked. They were a wild and often dishonest lot and stole as much of the supplies as they could. They had a trick of cutting the middle out of a pack of butter and leaving the two ends looking as if it was complete. They were not allowed to wear trousers in the monastery and some of them carried a leather bag between their legs in which they hid anything they could lay their hands on. And they used to take lots of things from simple villagers who wanted to make an offering for the monks' assembly. The servants, who lived outside the monastery, used to persuade the poor people to give them their presents of dry tea and flour, promising to take them in to the monastery; but they just pocketed the things.

The biggest and most powerful Dob-dob liked to take part in the tea-making by working the big churns in which the liquid tea is mixed with butter. They showed off their strength by thrusting the plunger of the churn down so hard that the butter spouted up to the ceiling. When they did this they wore leather aprons, because they were proud of their clothes and wanted to keep them clean. The kitchen servants, on the other hand, went about simply shining and stinking of old butter.

That business of tea serving led me into another fight. One day when I was doing it a group of bookmen monks whom I didn't know played a nasty trick by sticking a needle in the floor in front of them so that it would run into our bare feet. I was the first to be caught and when I saw them laughing I went to protest. They only laughed and used insulting words under their breath. I could not challenge them there, but I was ready for a fight and told them to wait outside. I was not sure that they would because bookmen usually avoid a fight if they can. But when I came out, there they were. When it was known there was to be a fight, a lot of people crowded round, including some senior Dob-dobs. Three or four of the bookmen came towards me together so I could not see which one to go for. The crowd would not have allowed the whole lot to attack me. That would have been against the custom and quite unfair. But the others distracted my attention so that their champion managed to hit me on the head with his key on the end of a strap. It was quite a severe wound which bled all over my face. I wiped the blood from my eyes and went for the man with my knife and got him in the groin. He fell down making a terrible fuss, and his friends ran to help him. None of them came anywhere near me. The crowd shouted encouragement to me and my Dob-dob friends standing in the background were very pleased. If the others had attacked me they would have come to my help, but it was the rule to leave fighters alone to settle their own business unless a regular group fight has been arranged. At all events my rival did not come back for more, so that was the end. The Proctors did not hear about the fight; or, if they did, they paid no attention. Probably everyone thought the bookmen had gone too far.

My father came to visit me that year for the performance of drama with dancing and singing, called Ache Lhamo. The dancers are specially trained groups of laymen from various parts of Tibet who came every year in late summer to perform for the Dalai Lama. After that they are allowed to go round to monasteries and private houses. The stories are told in a mixture of singing and recitative, rather like a simple kind of opera, and in between the scenes the company spin round in a circular dance to the accompaniment of a drum and cymbals. There are many comic interludes too. The party are all men or boys, but their performance as young or old women is often very clever.

Tibetans all love Ache Lhamo and would gladly sit all day, for several days running, to watch the show. Many of us know all the most famous songs and like to sing them at parties, and you might hear them sung, at the top of their voices, by people walking on the country roads.

Our khamtsen always engaged one of the best groups and fitted them out in good costumes which we kept for the occasion, for the dancers did not have any grand dresses of their own and it was the patron who provided them. We gave a great party from about 10 in the morning until sunset, to which we invited our relations and friends. They came in their smartest clothes and ornaments and sat round the courtyard where the dance was held. The Khamtsen provided lots of good tea, rice and pastries, and a bowl of curds which was the special dish of the festival. The college officials and teachers had a room in a gallery overlooking the courtyard, where they sat with their friends. We all took great pride and pleasure in entertaining our guests as well as possible, so it was a happy and light-hearted occasion.

After that I went home to help my father. It was not harvest time yet so I worked mostly with the animals. It was the time when Father had to send a couple of pigs as part of his dues to Sera. So they were killed by a hired man who did it very quickly by running a long sharp thorn into their hearts. Then he took the bodies to a hot spring some distance away where he left them until their hair came out. Later I put the bodies on a donkey and took them to the monastery official and at the same time I had several other loads which my father wanted taken to Lhasa. Sometimes I went with the ponies and donkeys to the river crossing to pick up loads, which traders had brought over by leather coracle, and took them on to Lhasa. That took about 2½ days and I might wait a day before finding any return loads, so I was quite busy. In the evenings I played the flute, or made ornaments for the plough cattle out of yak tails which I had brought from the drok. It had never been the same at home after my mother died. She had been so good at looking after us all. As it happened, that was the last time I was able to help my father at home because soon after that visit I took up an entirely new way of life.

Dote Chandzo, who still took an interest in me, knew a former Dob-dob of Sera who had given up his vows and had married and started a small restaurant in the city. He had a couple working for him, but neither was much good at cooking; and the owner and his wife spent most of their time making hats and boots in a room above the restaurant. Dote knew I could cook so he advised the owner to ask me to help him. I thought it was worth trying, so I agreed to try it and see how we got on. The place was on the south side of the city, near the Nepalese Officer's house, and it was run as a new sort of eating house for Lhasa, rather like a cafe. We served only Indian tea, which is easier to make well than good Tibetan tea, and it was very popular. Ours was particularly good, and cost a bit more than in other places where they were not so careful. We also served Tibetan meat dumplings called mo-mo and a special sort of fluffy pastry.We did not keep barley beer, but there were cigarettes on sale. The room was clean and comfortable. There was electric light in the street outside and some people had it in their houses, but it was expensive so we did very well with two pressure lamps. To amuse the guests there was a wireless set and two good carrom boards. Carrom is an Indian game played on a well-polished square board with a high rim round it and pockets at the four corners and in the sides. You have to hit large round counters into the pockets using another counter as striker and shooting with a flick of the finger. It was very popular and brought many people to the restaurant, where they often spent the greater part of the day.

I took over the cooking and management while the hired couple served and washed the dishes and cleaned the room. The first thing to be done was to get in fuel and water for the kitchen; then I had to buy meat, and get flour from the owner. Then I set about making dumplings for the guests who usually began to arrive about 10 or 11 in the morning. My dumplings were really very good and so our restaurant became one of the busiest in Lhasa, and I was kept hard at it making dumplings until about 8 at night. Then the owner, he was called Gyalpo Chandzo, and his wife and little daughter came down from their room and we had supper together after which I just rolled up in a blanket and slept there. I had to keep the accounts as well, and after a short time Gyalpo Chandzo trusted me completely and left the whole business in my hands. We usually took about £3 or £4 a day and he gave me about £3. a week and all the food I could eat, which was good pay for Lhasa. He was doing very well, too, with his business of making hats and boots in a smart, new fashioned pattern.

All sorts of people came to the restaurant: young noblemen who enjoyed carrom, schoolboys from a neighboring school during their break or on their way home, Khampas, Ladakhi Muslims, Nepalese and even some Chinese, mostly Muslims from Sining. Many of my Dob-dob friends came, too. I used to given them free tea sometimes, but the owner approved of that because it was the custom in many eating houses to give every visitor a free glass of *chang* as soon as he arrived. As we had no chang I gave them tea instead. And that made the visitors bring more and more of their friends.

I had trouble now and then, usually with a group of wild young men rather like "Teddy Boys", who seemed to have become rather numerous since the arrival of the Chinese. We called them Cutpurses, and that is what some of them were, especially if they found some ignorant and unsuspecting villager. However, sometimes they were caught out, like the one who cut a headsman's girdle because he saw it bulging, and found that what was in it was not money but a prayer book. Some of them acted as brokers in horse dealing, and expected a small tip from both buyer and seller. They were a dishonest and disreputable gang, and were quite crazy about going to the cinema which one of the nobles had opened in the city, and where Indian films were shown. They would steal from anyone to get money for their tickets. When they came to the restaurant they would spend hours eating and playing carrom and then might go off without paying. Eventually when their debts got too big I put up a list of their names and what they owed. That sometimes shamed them but once or twice I had to get hold of some of their possessions, a knife or a ring perhaps. One had a good bicycle which I seized, after getting permission from Gyalpo Chandzo. Other eating places suffered in the same way and the owner of one of them simply took the clothes of one of the gang and turned him out in his underpants. It was an advantage being a Dob-dob when dealing with such people. They knew I didn't mind a fight and that if they did me any harm my kyidu would be after them.

There was so much to do at the restaurant that I got no time to go home, but my father came to see me when he was in Lhasa. I kept my room in the khamtsen and was still on the college records, so I had to go there occasionally to call on the head of the college with a small present. When the Dalai Lama received all the monks of Sera, I joined my friends to go there and receive his blessing. And at the New Year I went to stay for a couple of days in my room, where Tashi Tshering helped me to decorate the altar with a sheep's head ornamented with butter, and a pot of green barley shoots. He and I went to call on the abbots and all the high lamas of the white monastery, as was customary, to offer a white scarf and a silver coin. In return they gave us a special sort of tea and traditional New Year dishes, pastries, meat sausage, and a cake of barley flour and butter. It took the whole of two days to pay all those calls. Then when I got back to Lhasa I attended the Great Prayer assembly; but I went only on two days. I didn't need the money now as I was so well paid.

In fact, I was really very hard worked, but I enjoyed it although I missed the exercises with the Dob-dobs. All the same, I saw my friends quite often when they came to Lhasa, and I got to know a great many people in the city. Gyalpo Chandzo was very pleased with me, especially when I told him I could do without the two helpers. Instead I took on a boy who was able to do all that was needed. I had quite a lot of money now and not much opportunity to waste it; but I bought good clothes, a short sword, a gold ring, more furniture for my room, and so on. Gyalpo often advised me to give up my vows, get married, and set up as a prosperous shopkeeper. However, I wanted to remain a monk and I had the idea that after a year or two I might go to Samye and start an eating house with my friend Tashi Tshering , who was a clever tailor and could run a small shop as well.

Living in Lhasa, I saw and heard a great deal more of the Chinese. Tibetans avoided talking to them as much as possible, and never tried to make friends except with the Muslims from Sining, who were really little better than prisoners. They had been brought to Tibet to labour on the heaviest tasks such as clearing building sites and making roads. They were very discontented and let us know secretly that they would join us against the communists if we managed to get the upper hand. The Chinese had barracks for their troops in strong positions all round the city.
One was opposite the Potala, and others near Drepung, Sera and Norbu Lingka. They had some difficulty at the camp near Sera which was near a small chapel of the protecting goddess Lhamo, and the Chinese found that every night they heard a woman walking though their lines, weeping and lamenting, but no one could ever get near her. It got so much on their nerves that they had to move their camp some distance away.

Most of the Chinese soldiers in Lhasa were quite young and

well-behaved. The people we did not like were the political workers who went about in the city. One day I went to the chinese barracks near Sera with a friend who was working in their kitchen. The food was quite good. There was a huge cauldron of rice and each man dipped his bowl into it, then took some meat from another cauldron and vegetables from another and wandered off by himself to eat it. Before they ate they lifted up their bowls and tapped them with their chopsticks and said some sort of slogan. They might come back for one or two more bowlsful. They trained very hard and drilled smartly, and I often saw them doing exercise in the morning dressed in shorts. In Lhasa the soldiers hardly left their barracks, though I believe that in some parts of the country they took over land and cultivated it.

One day I jumped up on the back of one of their military lorries in the street near our restaurant, thinking I would have a short ride. I was taken at once to an officer who asked me through an interpreter what I was doing. When I explained that I just wanted a ride, they took me to Dechen some miles away and then back to Lhasa.

Of course, our government officials had to work with the Chinese, but everyone knew that some of them were their favourites and were out for all they could get, while others did all they could to obstruct the Chinese plans. Ngapo Shappé, who had been captured by the Chinese when they first attacked Tibet and had been taken by them to China, was their chief favourite and was never seen without an armed Chinese escort. Others of those whom they liked had motor cars in which they were driven to meetings and parties; and the young nobles who were ready to work for them got motor bicycles as a reward. Hardly any Tibetan noble was able to keep horses now; and when they had to go to traditional ceremonies they had quite a lot of difficulty borrowing them.

There were many small ways in which the Chinese annoyed the ordinary people. They were like oil on paper; it starts with a small drop and spreads everywhere. They kept interfering with our customs and trying to make us change things; and there were constant announcements on noisy loudspeakers and lectures about the great things they were doing and how no one in the world was like them. There was a lot of clever talk against monks and monasteries, and they even criticized the Dalai Lama in an indirect way. Once they collected all the Lhasa beggars and offered them work for good pay. The beggars all said "No thank you, we are quite content as we are". Many townspeople were asked by the Chinese if they would send their children to China, where they would be very well educated. Only the poorest families were ready to allow that, so new Chinese schools were started in Lhasa. They killed all the dogs they could find in the streets. People said that they ate them, but it wasn't true that they ate the old mangy street dogs. They used to buy good dogs from the herdsmen and kill them for meat; you might see the bodies hanging upside down near their barracks. That disgusted and offended everybody. Another thing, too, that was offensive was their habit of burning great quantities of rubbish, old bones, rags and so on, which made an awful stench. Prices of course kept on going up, and even though the Chinese paid good wages to anyone who worked for them, no one was ever heard to speak in their favour except the half-Tibetans from Batang who had been under their influence for a long time, and whom they brought along as interpreters. The Chinese trusted them, but they did not trust all their own people, for they rounded up all the conjurors and acrobats, and men with performing animals who had followed them, and sent them off to China.

Now and then there was serious trouble. The Chinese kept on making roads, and for one of them they wanted to take land that ran through an estate belonging to Sera Me college. The steward there refused to allow this and there was a long argument. Eventually the Chinese came to see the steward one day and insisted that he should go to a party with them. He suspected they meant to kill him, so he went to the lavatory and loaded his revolver and then came back and shot the Chinese leader. There was a tremendous row, and he was imprisoned in Lhasa; but the abbots and monks of Mé college came into Lhasa and protested so strongly that he was released. That is just one example of how bad feeling was growing.

XII
THE UPRISING IN LHASA

Things got very much worse about a year after I had started working in the restaurant. The Dalai Lama and Panchen Lama had been taken on a visit to China some time before, and many Tibetans went with them. When the party came back they told us how badly the Chinese were treating the people of Amdo and Kham on the eastern borders of Tibet; and they said there was bound to be serious trouble. Before long reports began to reach Lhasa that fierce fighting had broken out, and that monasteries and villages were being bombed and shelled by Chinese troops, images and books had been destroyed, and a great many people tortured or killed. That made everyone in Lhasa angry and disturbed.

Support for the people of Amdo and Kham was organized in the city by a secret association called the Mimang -- the People's Party -- to which leading laymen, many Dob-dob, and some junior officials belonged. My employer, Gyalopo Chandzo, was a member and through him I sometimes met representatives of the fighters from Amdo and Kham who had formed a resistance army called the Chuzhi Gangdruk -- Four Rivers and Six Plateaux -- which is an old name for that part of the borderland. The Mimang took care to let people in Lhasa know what was happening and how the resistance army was putting up a brave fight and killing many Chinese. They did all they could to stop Tibetans fraternizing with the Chinese and to persuade parents not to send their children to the Chinese schools.

Feeling became much more bitter. The monks particularly disliked the new schools. Children who went there were fitted out free with clothes -- shorts, shirts, Chinese caps and so on -- and they were given a red scarf to wear round their necks. That annoyed the monks very much, because a red scarf used to be given to them by the Dalai Lama as a sign of his blessing. Whenever they saw a boy or girl wearing one they made them take it off; one Dob-dob even strangled a boy by twisting the scarf tightly round his neck. Girls who went about with the Chinese were threatened or beaten and some had their hair cut off. The huge posters of Mao and Stalin which the Chinese put up were regularly plastered with filth.

That all made the Chinese more and more hostile. They tried to get the abbots of Drepung and Sera to hand over all the weapons belonging to the monks there; but only a few were surrendered just to keep them quiet. They brought in some monks from Tashlhunpo, where they had influence through the Panchen Lama who was their favourite, and kept them as a sort of monk army in their barracks near Sera to make trouble for the Lhasa monks. There were more and more loud-speaker lectures; and the Chinese put up ugly figures near the Jokhang, supposed to be Americans, and said "Those are your friends. How do you like the look of them?". They gave film shows, boasting of their strength; but whenever Mao or anyone like that was seen the audience would whistle and pelt the screen with stones.

We heard from the Mimang that many of the Four Rivers and Six Plateaus army had had to leave their homes and were carrying on a guerilla fight against the Chinese in Tibet itself, cutting their supply lines and raiding their camps and convoys, even quite near Lhasa. Their leader Gompo Tashi, who was admired by everyone for his bravery and skill, came sometimes to our restaurant to meet Gyalpo Chandzo. He stayed in my father's house, too, when he went beyond Lhasa. The Chinese General in Lhasa wanted to have the Tibetan soldiers sent to fight the Chuzhi Gangdrug men, but our government would not agree. It seemed that trouble was brewing and, of course, people got more and more worried and excitable.

The New Year of 1959 was a time of great tension. Lhasa was full of monks as usual and the Dalai Lama himself came to the Jokhang and preached his New Year sermon. But, soon after he went back to the palace of Norbu Lingka, the city began to buzz with angry excitement. It was being said that the Chinese generals were putting pressure on the Dalai Lama to act against the Chuzhi Gangdrug, and that they wanted him to go to China. People feared he would then be in the Chinese' power and without proper protection. So when it was heard that the chinese commander had invited the Dalai Lama to go to a ceremony in their camp near Drepung, and had specially said that he should not bring a Tibetan escort with him, people were really alarmed for his safety.

News of the invitation was sent all round Lhasa at great speed. The Ragyabpas, the men who cut up the bodies of the dead, who were sometimes used as messengers by Lhasa officials, went from house to house telling the news, and there was great indignation everywhere. The abbots of Sera, of course, heard it and they sent men to call back their monks who were living outside the monastery. They specially wanted their strong men, the Dob-dob, back in case there was trouble. I packed up what I needed, borrowed a great sword from my master and hurried back to Sera.

It was quite a long time since I had been in the monastery, but my room was all right and I settled into it with some friends who came to join me. We were all angry and excited, and there was much talk of attacking the Chinese and protecting the Dalai Lama. The Dob-dob leaders went to demand rifles from the abbots. All they got was four hundred, which was not nearly enough. We also consulted the Karmashar oracle, who was the special seer of Sera. He came to the monastery and went into a trance, wearing his heavy robes and headdress; but whatever he said it didn't really help us much.

Next day I went off to Lhasa again with others who had not managed to get rifles; we meant to find out if we could get weapons there. First I went to Gyalpo Chandzo in the restaurant. He had been connected with the Mimang for a long time and was usually well informed and might be able to help. I found him wildly excited, brandishing a large mauser pistol and saying that everyone must go to Norbu Lingka to protect the Dalai Lama.

So we hurried along there with many other people. A huge crowd of men and women were packed solid in the wide road space in front of the palace, and a few minor officials were watching anxiously at the gates which were shut and had sentries posted at either side. Many of the crowd were weeping, and people were saying that if the Chinese came to take the Dalai Lama to their camp everyone would lie down in the road and stop the car. More and more people kept arriving, and there were shouts that the Chinese must leave Tibet and give us back our independence.

In the midst of this hubbub, two cars drove up from the direction of Lhasa and forced their way towards the gates as far as they could through the crowd. In one of them there was a lay official who was not immediately recognized. As he was in a Chinese car with a Chinese driver people thought that he had come to take the Dalai Lama away. In the excitement stones were thrown and the man was hit on the head. His party managed to take him away and we heard later that it was Sampho Shappé, a member of the Cabinet.

Soon after that a man arrived on motor bicycle and rode into the crowd trying to get to the palace. He was wearing a white shirt and dark trousers and a Chinese cap with a white face mask -- the sort the Chinese often used to keep out the dust. People surrounded him and asked where he was going. He seemed flustered and said "to Sera". That was obviously false because Sera was in the other direction. So the leaders of the crowd began to search him and felt what seemed to be grenades inside his shirt. He pulled out a revolver and fired two shots. Then someone recognized him as the brother and treasure of the Lama Phagpa La from Kham. Phagpa La was a well-known supporter and trusty of the Chinese. His brother was a monk, and usually wore monk's dress; in fact he had been wearing it that morning and had been seen leaving Norbu Lingka just as the crowd was beginning to gather. There were shouts of "Chinese spy!" and the word went round that he must be going in disguise to try to kill the Dalai Lama. In a flash the crowd set on him with stones and sticks and beat him to death.

The officials at the gate who heard the shouts and screaming of the wretched man, were told what had happened and they went in to report to the Dalai Lama and his ministers. Soon after, there was an announcement by loudspeaker from inside Norbu Lingka. Someone, I think it was Surkhang Shappe, said that the Dalai Lama was not going to the Chinese camp. There was great shout of relief. Then the speaker asked us all to go away quietly. He or someone else also said that Phagpa La's brother was a Chinese agent.

Once they were reassured that the Dalai Lama would not go to the Chinese camp many of the crowd began to go back to Lhasa. They took with them the body of the dead man which they dragged all round the Jokhang and the centre of Lhasa. But others stayed, especially the Mimang leaders, and made barricades round Norbu Lingka because no one trusted the Chinese not to come secretly and take the Dalai Lama by force. The soldiers of the Tibetan army also came from their barracks and took up positions round Norbu Lingka while others went and occupied the Potala and the Chakpori hill near it.

All this time there was no sign of any activity by the Chinese. They must have been discussing, planning and making preparations, and as we went back to the city we could see guns at the ready and men with rifles forming up in the big camp and barracks near the Potala. We were all wild with excitement and fury and, although we knew the Chinese were too powerful, we were quite ready to fight to the death rather than give in.

I went back to Sera with my friends and we lay talking most of the night, wondering what was going to happen. For the next six days we were forbidden by the abbots to leave the monastery but we got news that Lhasa was in a state of great tension and disturbance and we could see much activity in the Chinese camp at Trapchi. The news was that the Chinese were moving their big guns into position and training them on all the important places -- Norbu Lingka, the Potala, Chakpori, Drepung, and Sera. More troops were said to be arriving every day. A great number of Tibetans, Mimang, Khampas, and ordinary people of Lhasa, stayed on guard round Norbu Lingka. The Dalai Lama's ministers asked them to remove the barricades and go away, but they were now in such a state of anger and suspicion that they refused to go unless the Chinese took down the barricades they had been building in Lhasa and drew back their guns. We were all on tenderhooks and it seemed that there was bound to be an explosion.

I heard later what set off the explosion, though we did not know for certain at the time. One afternoon — I think it was the 26th day of the Tibetan month — the Chinese for some reason, perhaps as a warning, dropped a few shells into Norbu Lingka. The Dalai Lama and his advisers took this as a sign that they meant to attack the Tibetans who were defending the place, and perhaps destroy Lhasa too. It was decided that they should leave the Palace and take refuge somewhere else. His Holiness has described in his book how he escaped by night and eventually reached India after a hard and dangerous journey.

It was some days before the Chinese were sure that the Dalai Lama had left Lhasa but the rumour had reached us almost at once. Gyalpo Chandzo knew, and I had a message from him. At all events there was still much uncertainty; and the Tibetan guards and ordinary people stayed where they were, all round the palace, until the Chinese came to the conclusion that the Dalai Lama had gone. Then on the

28th of the month they opened a furious fire on Norbu Lingka and the Tibetans all round it. Their big guns caused terrible slaughter among the crowd, I was told.

We in Sera were alarmed by the outbreak of firing and could see explosions of dust and clouds of smoke from the direction of Lhasa. Then suddenly with a series of crashes three shells in rapid succession hit the hillside just behind Sera. Most of us were already outside, watching the explosions in Lhasa, and we quickly took cover in ditches and ravines. There was a short silence and then a clamour of angry shouting. We thought we were being attacked and began to look for a way to fight back.

When no more shells fell and we could see no Chinese troops approaching from Trapchi, we calmed down a bit. The Chinese certainly had spies in the monastery. There were always a few monks who started stories obviously inspired by them; and now word began to go round that the shells were only a warning from the Chinese that we should stay where we were and not go into Lhasa. In spite of these rumours most of us were furious. We could hear firing from Lhasa and see the shells bursting. We wanted to do something active.

A powerfully built young monk stood out as leader. He was not a Dob-dob but a man of learning and authority; in fact he was a Geshé, a teacher, of the Pompara Khamtsen. He proposed that we should go to the Potala and get weapons from the arms store there. "Hands up anyone who will come with me" he said. That was something we had learnt from the Chinese who taught us that way of voting. About four hundred of us, mostly Dob-dob, but not all, volunteered to follow him and we set off at once without going back to collect food or anything.

Another group planned to attack the Tashilhunpo monks in their quarters near the Trapchi barracks, and prevent them either by force or persuasion from helping the Chinese.

From Sera you can see the Potala a couple of miles away. Between it and the monastery is a stream running inside a high sand embankment. Our party made as fast as we could for the shelter of that embankment while the Chinese in the Trapchi barracks opened fire on us. No one was hit; and as soon as we were under cover we could hurry along quite safely until we came in sight of another Chinese camp which they had made near a pleasant tree-shaded lake on the north side of the Potala. As soon as we came in sight they opened up on us with machine guns but we still had quite good cover and, again, there were no casualties.

There were some Tibetan soldiers in the Potala itself and when they saw what was happening, they fired at the Chinese camp and distracted their attention from us. We lay low while this was going on; and after a time we saw three fast light armoured cars rushing towards the Potala from the Trapchi barracks. I suppose the Chinese in the other camp had called them up. By a great stroke of luck the Tibetans in the Potala hit one of the armoured cars, probably with a mortar. It burst into flames and the other two turned and hurried back

That gave us the chance to go on cautiously until we came opposite Kundeling monastery where we crossed into the shelter of a poplar grove, through which we got unobserved on to the steep road leading up to the north gate on the Potala hill. We rushed upwards, taking cover from the parapets on both sides of the road, and found Tibetan sentries guarding the gate. They let us in and told us where the rifles and ammunition were stored. The place was at the west end of the Potala, on the south side, completely exposed to sight and well within range of the Chinese in their camp to the south of the Potala. No one knew who had the key of the store so we decided we would just have to break open the doors with our swords and wooden poles or anything else we could find.

The soldiers said we simply hadn't a chance because the place was covered by the Chinese guns. All the same, Pompara Geshé said there was nothing for it but to take the risk. He called again for volunteers and we were all ready to try.

The rifle store was in a strong white stone tower standing a bit apart from and in front of the main building. We had to run down the wide, slippery stone stairway leading down from a door on the south east end of the Potala, then across a courtyard to the door which was on one side of the tower and partly sheltered from the Chinese. They opened up with mortars and rifles as soon as they saw us on the stairway but we got down safely, broke the doors open, collected many hundreds of rifles and dashed back taking cover as well as we could from the stone parapets of the stairway.

Ammunition next. That was much harder as the store was more exposed. We had to make a line on the stairway and pass the boxes from hand to hand up to the gate. By then much of the parapet had been shattered by mortar fire but we squatted down as low as we could and pulled and shoved the boxes from one to the other. Several of us were wounded and it was frightening at first to hear the bullets screaming past and hitting the walls with a smack; but only one of us was killed, a young boy from Lhasa who had insisted on joining us and had worked with great spirit and cheerfulness.

Eventually we were all back in cover, well supplied with rifles and ammunition but tired and shaken after all the effort and excitement. It was still some hours before sunset and, although we had been on the go for a long time, we didn't feel hungry so we took a rest, looked after the wounded, and discussed our situation. In most of the rooms and big halls of the Potala there were parties of women and children who had been sent there for safety; but now the Chinese were shelling the building from time to time and several of these unfortunate people had been killed and many wounded. There was blood, dust and confusion everywhere and much weeping and lamenting; but there were many brave women and boys to. Some monks of the Dalai Lama's monastery in the Potala -- the Namgye Tratsang -- were there but they were mostly shocked and useless. There was little we could do for anyone. There were no bandages, no water, no tea and no food. We could only try to encourage and comfort them. It wasn't easy. Shells continued to hit the Potala from time to time and we could hear firing all round and loudspeakers shouting out to everyone to surrender. The strongly built temple on the top of the Chakpori, which had a solid round tower, was held by Tibetan soldiers who had helped us by firing at the Chinese camp when we were running up to the Potala and when we were getting the rifles and ammunition. About midday the Chinese turned their heavy fire on that temple and more or less blew it to bits. The Tibetans had to clear out, but later made a brave attempt to reoccupy it, only to be shelled out of it again. Kundeling monastery, not far from it, suddenly went up in flames and we could see the monks running in terror and being shot down as they ran.

Our soldiers and the Chuzhi Gangdrug fought with great bravery. They had only light mortars and rifles but they were quite fearless and took great risks. One particular hero was a little cripple fellow who used to play the bagpipes in the Police band. He was well known as a cheerful joker, but that day he was a hero. He had absolutely no fear and was rushing about attacking the Chinese with a rifle whenever he could see them. He was shouting, laughing and cheering the others on. I suppose he was killed; he could hardly escape death the way he was fighting.

Up in the Potala there was not much we could do though we shot at any Chinese troops we could see. Our leader suggested that we should go down and attack the Chinese camp on the north of the Potala; but a regular soldier of the Trapchi regiment stopped us. He caught our clothes and wept and said it was a complete waste of our lives and meant certain death as the Chinese had the approaches covered with much better weapons than we had. So we decided to wait until it was dark when we could move about more freely.

Now, waiting for night to fall, we felt hungry and thirsty; but none of us had brought anything to eat and the unhappy people in the Potala had practically nothing for themselves. Not one of the chapel keepers or attendants of the Potala could be found, so we wandered round the great building, into a maze of rooms where I had never been before, up and down dark passages and wooden stairways, into great halls and small rooms, into the Cabinet room where the ministers met. We went even into the tomb chapels of the Dalai Lamas, the great hall with a towering gilded chöten containing the body of the late Dalai Lama, and the long dark shrine where the bodies of many of the earlier Lamas are entombed. All the precious objects, the gold and jewels, bowls, lamps, ornamental crowns, everything, were standing there untended. There was no caretaker to be seen. We went also into the private rooms of the Dalai Lama himself at the highest point of the east end of the Potala hoping somewhere to find flour, tea or butter. There was nothing; only gold and silver cupstands, jade bowls, porcelain, silks, images of precious metal decorated with jewels; but no food. So we took from the many altars, the butter and flour offerings and drank the water from the ritual offering bowls. None of us had ever done such a thing before or even heard of it being done, but no one thought there was any wrong in it. We were fighting for the Dalai Lama and our faith and those things we took were never regarded as anything but pious offerings. We touched nothing else.

I am told the Chinese have said that they did no damage to the Potala and that some foreign visitors, who went to Lhasa some years later, said it was unharmed. That is not true. I saw it myself. The Zhol at the foot of the Potala hill was flattened; the Namgyé Tratsang at the west end was in ruins and there were gaping holes at several places along the front. I saw, too, the bodies of people who had been killed inside the building and many more all round it.

That terrible day seemed endless. We were inactive but quite unable to rest or relax. Late in the afternoon we saw shells begin to fall on Sera which had been left alone for most of the day, so that added to our anxiety. Night came at last; and as soon as we dared, we found our way with difficulty along the dark passages of the Potala and moved silently out of the north door and down the hills, where we quickly crossed over into the shelter of the sand embankment again. Searchlights were swinging over the plain from the Chinese camps, and more than once we were dazzled as they caught us, and the Chinese fired at us again. We lay down and tried to crawl away. One of us was killed and several more were hit; but at last we reached home.

XIII
FLIGHT TO INDIA

I went to my room with some friends. We had been talking in the Potala about what a good meal we would have when we got back to the monastery and now we brought out all our best stores of tea, meat, butter and flour and prepared what should have been a wonderful feast. But the reaction to the excitement, the sadness and exhaustion was so great that none of us could eat. We couldn't even drink the really delicious tea — the very best sort that we hardly ever had except at festivals — so we mixed it with tsampa and kept it as our rations for the next day. Then we tried to sleep.

It was not a peaceful night. The Chinese bombarded the monastery at intervals and we never knew when or where to expect the next shell. As each one fell, the dogs howled dismally and the horses in the stables neighed and stamped in terror. During the night the leaders of various groups held discussions, planning what to do next. Dote Chandzo had been in touch with the Khampas of the Chuzhi Gangdrug army and had been told that the Dalai Lama was making for Tawang, a monastery just inside in Indian border, near Bhutan. He proposed to take the young Sharpa Lama there too. It was decided to make up quite a small party and to leave before daylight, taking a track running just behind Sera into a rather deserted, steep glen leading over a high pass into the Phenpo valley. It would have been madness to use the direct road through Lhasa. Sharpa Lama liked me, and Dote Chandzo regarded me as brave and hardy, so they woke me up and told me to get ready to go with them. There were about ten people in our party including the Rampa Kalon Lama — the monk Cabinet Minister — who was the Sharpa Lama's uncle. He had taken refuge in a small hermitage near Sera. We at once gathered all the supplies we could, took such valuables as we could carry, and buried the rest in the floors of our rooms and courtyards of the monastery. We loaded up our horses and mules, ready for the start; all round us other parties were making the same sort of arrangements.

It was still dark when we left the monastery. Sharpa Lama, The Kalon Lama, the Chandzo, and all the rest of us were in lay dress and were well armed with rifles, revolvers and swords. The Lama rode his favourite horse but there were not enough riding animals for the rest of us. In fact there were only four between the whole party.

In spite of all the exertion of the previous day I was not feeling tired or afraid, but I wondered whether I should ever see Sera again.

The tracks ran at first up the sandy valley where we Dob – dob used to exercise. It soon grew steeper and rougher, but we pushed on fast as the light became stronger, so it did not take us long to reach the pass about 20 miles from Sera. We threw stones on to the cairn at the summit and moved quickly down into the Phenpo valley as the sun came up. We were heading for a small estate near the Nalenda monastery, which belonged to the Labrang. The usual road would have been by the Phenpo Go pass, but that would not have been safe because there were Chinese outposts on that road. So when we reached the Phenpo valley we had to turn downstream for some miles and then climb up the hill – side again to the estate.

As soon as the farmers knew that the Sharpa Lama had arrived, they all came to make offering to him and to get his blessing. Many were weeping bitterly, and saying that, although they did not dare to try to escape, they would give everything they had to help their Lama. We rested there and had something to eat, and those of us who had not had horses now got them from the villagers. They were very generous in giving us the best of everything.

After a while we went off down the valley, where we found a big party of Khampa soldiers of the Chuzhi Gangdruk encamped. It was sad to see that although some of them were quiet and kind, most were giving the Phenpo farmers a lot of trouble, taking what they needed by force or threats — horses, flour, butter — and were even carrying off the girls. They stopped us and told us we must stay with them and add to their strength, for they meant to go back to Lhasa and attack the Chinese. But we did not like the way they were behaving and decided to go our own way. Then they seized our horses, threatened to shoot us, and more or less made us prisoners. We nearly came to blows but that would not have done any good, so we just had to stay. But we were determined to get away from them as soon as possible.

The Khampas' headquarters was in a fine old estate house belonging to the Lhalu family, and before long it must have been spotted by a
Chinese aeroplane which appeared about midday and flew over quite
low, machine – gunning everything in sight. A lot of sheep and cows
were killed, but no one was hurt. The Khampas fired back at the plane
but didn't hit it. The pilot turned back and dropped some bombs on the
house without doing much damage.

The disturbance allowed us to get away; and when it was dark we
crossed the Phenpo river to a small nunnery on the other side. The nuns
gave us shelter and food and asked to join our party and escape to India.
They were clever and brave for such simple – seeming women, and
they had managed to hide a number of good mules in their stables.

Next morning the aeroplane came back and we could see it machine –
gunning and bombing the neighbourhood of the Lhalu house again,
but it did not come near the nunnery. As soon as we could we set off
again. This time we left the Kalon Lama with his two servants. He was
an old man and not able to face the long journey to India, so he decided-
to go to a small estate nearby and take shelter there. Our numbers
were slightly increased by half a dozen of the nuns who insisted on coming
with us. The older ones stayed behind in the nunnery.

We went down the Phenpo valley to its junction with the Lhasa river
and forded the main river just above that point. The water was not very-
deep but was flowing fast. A great many people were crossing there,
for many parties had fled from Lhasa into Phenpo by a number of different
passes. Most of us got over safely, but I saw one poor little boy monk
swept away and drowned. After crossing the river we turned downstream
to Dechen Dzong. That took us closer to Lhasa, but, as we had not enough
good horses and mules for the journey, the plan was that some of us should
go to the estates of the Shasur family, which were even nearer Lhasa,
and collect as many animals as possible.

There was another camp of the Chuzhi Gangdruk at Dechen, and
a great crowd of refugees who had crossed the river near Lhasa and
were uncertain what to do next. We left Sharpa Lama and some others
there and went as fast as possible to Shasur's estates. They were uncom-
fortably close to Lhasa but at least we were on the opposite bank. The
noise of shooting was still going on and dust and smoke could be seen
all round the city. There was no temptation to delay so we collected all
the good horses and mules we could find and came away with enough

for us all.

There were so many people at Dechen including the Khampas and as we were afraid they might be troublesome and try to stop us or take our horses we pushed on at once to another estate at the foot of the hill where Ganden monastery is situated in a sheltered fold of the mountain. About two miles from our halting place there was a camp of Chinese soldiers who had their guns trained on Ganden in order to terrorize the monks and keep them quiet; but fortunately no one paid any attention to us so we spent a reasonably quiet night.

The next day we left very early and hurried along the road towards the east. It is the broad highroad the Chinese made for their jeeps and lorries. There were crowds of Tibetans riding or walking in an effort to get away from Lhasa. Many were tired, footsore and weeping. Fortunately no Chinese planes or armoured cars came that day and we soon turned off the main road onto a rough track leading southward to Okha. This was much the same road as I had travelled on my happy journeys to and from the Drok in Dagpo and we were heading for the same place, because it was an estate of the Labrang. As we went some soldiers, who had joined in with us, blew up the bridges to prevent the Chinese following with jeeps. There were fewer people on this route and much of the country was wild and bleak.

It took us about six days to reach Drilung estate in Dagpo, travelling by little used tracks through difficult country and cold weather, and spending the night usually in small villages. There were groups of Khampas here and there but we avoided them as far as possible, particularly as we heard rumours that parties of Chinese had disguised themselves as Khampas and were capturing many of the fugitives round about Dechen and beyond. The nuns kept up with us bravely. They lamented a bit; but they were a great help wherever we halted, looking after the horses, boiling water and so on.

After a fast and tiring journey we were ready for a rest at Drilung estate. It was very different now, coming back there, after about eight years, to where I had been so happy. The farmers and herdsmen were very sad to see their Lama having to leave his monastery, and they did all they could to help. The Lama himself, although he was only about 12, was full of spirit. He never complained of the hardship and was always careful to see that his favourite horse was properly fed, and would share his own barley meal with it.

We didn't dare risk staying long, as rumours kept arriving that the Chinese were pursuing the refugees. So when we had got together fresh supplies of food and changed some of our old and tired animals for better, we set off again. We headed down the Okha river towards the valley of the Tsangpo — the Brahmaputra — which was two days march away. Then we followed the great river upstream to a place where there was a ferry. We crossed in a big wooden boat and so arrived at Tsetang. There were many prosperous traders there, Nepalese and Ladakhis as well and there were two big monasteries. The Chinese kept a strongly fortified outpost there because it was an important town. When we arrived we found a big battle going on between the Chuzhi Gangdruk and the Chinese. We could not avoid being drawn into the battle, as the Khampa and Amdowa fighters were controlling all traffic and ordering all men with weapons to stay and join in the attack.

There seemed a good hope of wiping out the Chinese camp, which might otherwise be a danger to Tibetans trying to escape through Tsetang, so we gladly joined up with the Chuzhi Gangdruk. They fed us well and they were very good at military matters, but I am sorry to say there was no genuine good feeling between us. Amdowas and Khampas are famous for their independent, hot – tempered and rather rough nature and, although I got on well with many of them individually, when they were all together they were too wild and domineering and did not treat us with consideration. But they were tremendously brave and they had good reason to be fierce and cruel, for they had lost everything in their homeland and had been fighting the Chinese in difficult conditions for about three years.

Here at Tsetang they had surrounded the camp, where the Chinese had dug themselves in in a series of tunnels and only came out at night to get water. When they did that, they used strong searchlights to dazzle us, and they let off a great fusillade of rifle shots as protection for their watering parties. A lot of harmless refugees were killed or wounded in that way.

A Chinese who had been an officer in the Communist army, but had become disgusted and had deserted them, gave us great help. There were several Chinese who did the same; but that man was the best. He was an experienced commander and an expert with machine guns. There was also a Dob – dob warrior from Drepung, called Wangdi — a huge noisy swashbuckler but absolutely fearless. He had eaten a printed image of one of the terrible Protectors of Religion in order to make himself fierce. Those are objects one should wear as amulets but to eat them is a dangerous thing for it takes away the hope of a good rebirth for many ages to come.

A plan was made to attack the Chinese camp in two detachments, one under the Chinese officer and the other under Wangdi. I was put under Wangdi and we all surrounded the camp and opened heavy fire on it with rifles and mortars. That kept the Chinese down, and we were able to rush the place all together. Wangdi found an entrance and a party of Khampas followed him in and killed about 600 Chinese. Quite a lot of them surrendered and came out with their hands up, but there was no way of keeping prisoners so they were all shot. Wangdi himself was killed when he forced his way into one of the underground tunnels and was surrounded by the enemy.

The rest of the Chinese kept up a brave fight and managed to get machine guns trained on us, so that we had to retire. We attacked again, but their fire was too powerful. Next day a large number of fresh Chinese troops appeared from somewhere and saved the situation for their fellows.

The Chuzhi Gangdruk men, when they saw they could not wipe out the camp, simply took to their horses — of course they had the best — and rode off without telling us, leaving us to fend for ourselves. That was the sort of treatment that made for bad feeling.

We had to get out of Tsetang as quickly as we could in case the new Chinese troops came round looking for arms. We spent a night in Tsetang after the Chuzhi Gangdruk had left and set out again early the next day. The nuns were no longer with us. They had decided to stay in On, on the other side of the river because they were exhausted and could not go further. They generously gave us their good horses, some clothes, and a supply of tea and food.

The first day out of Tsetang something happened that I shall never forget. We were riding along a hillside when I saw a fine horse standing by a great boulder some way below us. We needed good horses so I clambered down to get it while the others rode on. To my surprise I saw lying in the shelter of the boulder a woman wearing the dress of a Lhasa lady of some wealth. There was a big knife sticking in her left breast; her face was white and blood was pouring from her mouth. She was unconscious and obviously could not live, as the blood was pumping out in great gushes. I felt great pity and though I could not leave her like that; I wanted to end her suffering. It is a terrible sin to take life but we are taught, too, that we must always show compassion; and something told me what I must do. I prayed quickly; then took my rifle and shot her.

At the noise of the shot the horse took fright and ran off. I could not catch it.

When I got back to our party and they asked about the firing I told them what had happened. The Chandzo blamed me and said it was the worst possible sin; but the Lama and others said it might have been the right thing to do. Somehow what they said did not worry me. I don't suppose I could have done such a thing if the life of all of us had not been so greatly upset by the violence and bloodshed of the last few weeks; but felt quite calm when I did it and, although it makes me sad to think of the poor woman, I feel no guilt about it.

XIV
TAWANG

So we went on, day after day; each was much the same as the last- and I was too worried and tired to pay much attention to the country we were passing through. It was not really cold, except for some nights in the highest places. Usually we slept in a village, perhaps in a small chapel; the people always showed respect and affection for Sharpa Lama and brought us supplies and told us the best routes through the quietest and most lonely parts of the country so that there would be less risk of being seen by the enemy. Often they lent us horses for part of the journey.

We saw other refugees on the way from time to time; but fortunately no Chinese troops and no aeroplanes came our way. Some of the refugees were Khampa soldiers, who managed to kill a lot of wild pigs in one place and we got some meat from them. We usually got enough to eat for ourselves, but the going was hard and there was not enough fodder for our horses and mules. The weakest of them died long before we reached the Indian frontier. In fact we were down to three by then. The Lama's horse survived, and he and Dote Chandzo usually rode; the other horse carried supplies and baggage. We had to leave the saddles of the dead horses by the road and make packs of what we needed and carry as much as we could on our backs. Other people were doing the same. There were many dead animals and all sorts of goods left abandoned by the side of the road. One day we found a machine gun by the tracks. A Khampa soldier had probably got tired of carrying it. It was no use to us, but a sack of rice we found was very welcome. Our ordinary food was mostly dried meat and tsampa, with tea perhaps, when we halted.

There were all sorts of rumours in the villages and among the refugees. No one knew whether the Chinese were pursuing us or whether we would find Chinese patrols near the border. There was said to be a big Chinese barracks near Tsona Dzong so we avoided going anywhere near there; but there was the danger that the troops from that camp might be on the move.

After about a week we came, at last, safely to the last range of mountains before the Indian border and the way to Tawang. We found we had to cross a high and troublesome pass, the Mago La, and there, unfortunately, we ran into heavy snow. It fell the whole day while we were climbing up to the pass and we had to spend the night in deep snow before we could reach the summit. The next day it was so deep that we could move only very slowly, after some of the refugees had driven yaks and mules ahead to stamp it down. Sometimes not even the animals could go until some of us had laid our cloaks on the snow and crawled over them to press it down a bit. Many people were completely buried in the snow and in some places when a yak fell in it disappeared right up to the tips of its horns. I had never seen snow like that.

Now the Chuzhi Gangdruk showed up at their best. They were strong and tough and seemed quite tireless in pressing on with the track through the snow. Most of them had all sorts of possessions which they threw away to make it easier to move. The first thing to go was great bundles of Chinese paper money which was now, of course, useless and which they hurled about in handfuls.

After two days of strenuous, exhausting climbing in cold wet snow we struggled up to and over the pass. Almost at once we found ourselves, to our relief, in a different country. It was suddenly damp and warm; there were trees of a new kind, rhododendrons of many sorts with bright flowers, and birds were singing. I remember it well, but at the time I had no heart to think how beautiful it was. In fact we ordinary Tibetans did not seem to pay much attention to such things. I often hear my friends in this country saying how lovely the trees are, or the flowers, or bird song, and these are certainly good things, but until lately I did not have the habit of noticing them much.

When we reached the other side of the pass we supposed we were safely in India but we went on slowly for several days without meeting anyone. There were many wild animals in the wooded valley through which we travelled and we were able to kill some deer. Eventually we came to an outpost of Indian frontier guards who stopped us. There were six soldiers there, living in a hut with a telephone connected with their headquarters at Tawang. Some of our party knew a little Hindi and the Indians had men from Tawang with them who could act as interpreters. We found out that the Dalai Lama and his party had got safely to Tawang, and that quite a lot of other refugees had arrived before us by the same route. The Indians told us that we would have to wait where we were until they got permission for us to go on to Tawang.

The place we had to stay in was in sight of the high snow peaks of Tibet but was damp and warm and full of flies and leeches. There was plenty of firewood but we had hardly any food left. Our supply of tsampa and butter ran out almost at once; but we still had tea which we brewed up very strong and refreshing. There was a kind of ragwort growing all round so we gathered that and other green things and cooked them; but they were not very good. The Indian guards were very friendly and helpful but they had no supplies to spare. They said they would send for some from Tawang; and they spoke cheerfully to us and gave us biri to smoke.

As it seemed we might have to wait there some time, we asked for permission to hunt some of the wild animals and the guards allowed us to do so, provided we didn't kill any cows. So I went out and managed to shoot a big deer; another of our party got a musk deer, so that gave us plenty of meat and the ragwort and dandelions tasted better with that.

By now many other parties of refugees had arrived and were also kept waiting for leave to go on. No one had any food left and things were getting difficult, when some Indian aeroplanes arrived and dropped all sorts of supplies for us — rice, dahl, ghee and even goats — on parachutes. We were delighted and very grateful, and we divided the supplies between us fairly. The parachutes were useful, too, for we made tents out of them and were able to settle down more comfortably than before, when we had only shelters made of branches.

After about a week we were told we might go on to Tawang. It was four days march, rather slow going in hilly country with steep rough paths, and warmer than we were used to. Most of us were on foot, but Sharpa Lama's horse was still going well. The Tawang people who came with us as guides — Monbas we call them — were, of course quite used to the conditions and moved far more easily than we did. We felt less tense now; there was no fear that anyone was chasing us so there was no hurry. There was plenty of wood, mostly bamboo, for making fires at our night halts; we had enough to eat, and parachute tents; we even got used to the leeches which were not too bad at that time of year; and in the evenings we relaxed and chatted or played games.

Before reaching Tawang we met a party of Chuzhi Gangdruk

men who asked us to give them our rifles, saying they were going back to fight the Chinese. They had rifles and ammunition of their own, so we told them we had no government now and meant to keep our rifles as long as we could; perhaps we should get orders somewhere from the Dalai Lama or his ministers. However, some of the more timid refugees did give up their rifles when the Khampas threatened them.

It was exciting to reach Tawang at last and our hearts were thrilled to see again a large Tibetan monastery sheltered on a hillside looking over a wide valley. The Abbots were from Drepung, but most of the monks were Monbas — simple, friendly people who made us welcome and gave us food. It was mostly maize and buckwheat, which we did not much like, but we were, after all, more or less beggars. There was rice and tsampa and butter to be had there but it was very expensive. The Monbas spoke a rather different Tibetan from ourselves but we could understand each other all right.

Tawang monastery, though it looked grand from outside, was dismal dirty and ruinous inside. Rain had leaked down many of the frescoed walls and the place was damp and musty. There were two incarnate Lamas there, each with his own Labrang, but the whole place seemed rather poor and neglected. There was, also, a great stone building which had been a prison but it, too, was tumbling down.

We heard that the Dalai Lama and his party had stayed in Tawang for a few days and then gone on to the plains of India, where, we supposed, we would follow him. In the meantime there were a great many Tibetans camped on the slopes below the monastery and Indian officials were busy making lists, finding out who everyone was and where they came from. They took our rifles and gave us receipts for them but, of course, we never saw them again and might just as well have given them to the Chuzhi Gangdruk.

The Indians must have taken a lot of trouble to help us, for every three days aeroplanes flew over and dropped supplies. The officials were pleased with the way we Tibetans organized parties to collect the things and guard them. We arranged, too, to sort them out and distribute them fairly without taking anything secretly.

We lived for about a month at Tawang and seemed almost to be settling down there. Many of the local people and the monks of the monastery came to visit Sharpa Lama and to get his blessing. They brought him offerings of food and money, but we all wanted to find some way of making our own living. Dote Chandzo had brought a lot of Tibetan currency notes with him and was very sad when he found they were no use at all in India. If he had been more experienced, he would have brought some of the gold which he buried under the floor of his room in the Labrang. I am afraid he will never see that again. We sold the remaining horses, which the Monbas were glad to buy. The country was not really suitable for horses because of flies and leeches, and the fodder was not what they were used to; but the Monbas thought it a distinction to own a Tibetan horse and gave us a good price.

I had very little money of my own, but I had some valuables which I sold one by one — a charm box of silver and turquoise, a sword, a bronze choten, and my cloak. That provided enough money to buy things to supplement the rations we got, so we were well enough fed. But most of us wanted work not only to make a little money but also to keep us occupied. First I bought a good kukri and went out to cut bamboo which I sold as fodder. Then an Indian, whom we called Babu La, who was doing some sort of job there, took me on as a servant. He spoke Tawang dialect fairly well, so we got on all right. I used to clean his house, make tea for him and so on. He gave me food, cigarettes, good trousers and shoes and some money. He had a Monba girl living with him, but there was a very beautiful Tibetan girl among the refugees whom he wanted very badly. He said he would give me 100 rupees if I would get her to come and live with him. I spoke to her about it, but she was very angry and would have nothing to do with Babu La. Her father came to me later and scolded me.

Some of the Monba girls were really lovely. I got to know one who took a liking to me and asked me to her father's house, where I was kindly received and asked to stay. I stayed there about three weeks and worked for the family in their rice fields. I even ploughed the fields, though a monk is not supposed to do that: but we were refugees now and others were doing the same. The father said "Why not give up your vows, marry the girl and stay here as my son-in-law?". He needed someone strong to help him, as he had no son. The girl was quite ready to marry me. She was cheerful and pretty, but the place was so dirty. The wood of the house smelt damp, rotten and musty and the girl was dirty, too; she never washed even her hands and she was rather smelly. So although I kissed her quite often, I was not really tempted to give up my vows, marry her, and settle for the rest of my life in Tawang. Some of refugees, including some Dob-dob, did marry Monba girls and stay there. It was a pleasant place in many ways but Dote Chandzo advised me not to think of staying; and I think he was right. I wonder what happened to my Tibetan friends who stayed there, when the Chinese came and captured Tawang a few years later.

After about a month we were told we could go on into India. Before we left we were given some sort of injection and a large red pill. I suppose they were to prevent cholera and malaria but we were not told. There were plenty of mosquitos at Tawang, but there did not seem to be any fever there. In fact, it was a healthy place, the water was good and very few of the refugees fell ill.

So once again we set out for our next goal — Bomdi La, where we were told there was a big camp and the start of a motor road to the plains. We still had three mules, so the Lama was able to ride. The rest of us went on foot carrying all the baggage we had left. We cast lots for the various loads. I got one of dried meat, which smelt very badly in that warm climate but was useful as rations for the journey. The road was a rough track that climbed up and down steep hills from one valley to the next. It was either stony or muddy, and there were leeches and flies every-where in the hot damp forest. The going was hard and tiring and my boots didn't last long so that I finished up with only one and the other foot bare. Others who had started barefoot suffered much worse as our feet cracked and bled. I don't know why it was so much worse than in Tibet where we could walk on bad roads without such trouble; perhaps the damp and the heat were to blame. Most of us had sold our good Tibetan dress in Tawang and we certainly did not miss our heavy cloaks here. It was so hot that we stripped to a little loin cloth and plodded along almost naked. That amused us for it is something we don't do in Tibet.

We had food enough and there was no need to hurry but we all wanted to get on to India. None of us knew exactly what we hoped to do there but we thought "Let's get to India, surely we shall find work there". So when, after nine or ten days we reached Bomdi La and knew that Assam was quite near, many of us climbed up a little hill near the camp and saw below us the vast flat plains stretching far away out of sight and the river gleaming there. We all shouted with delight.

At Bomdi La we sold our three mules to the Indian Army for 600/; and after a short time most of us were sent off to walk for two days down the road to Misamari in the plains, where a camp had been set up for refugees from Tibet. Old people and the sick were taken there in lorries and the Lama and Chandzo were taken in a jeep.

XV
THE BIGGEST BLOW OF ALL

The camp at Misamari to which we were taken was a great enclosure on bare sandy ground; it was quite without trees and there was no shade of any sort. We were directed to one or other of many long rows of bamboo huts, each of which could hold about sixty people. The Indian officials, helped by Tibetan interpreters, made lists of our names and where we had come from. We were medically inspected. Then we were given soap and a towel and told to take a bath, which we did in a river that ran quite near the camp and was very dirty and sandy. Our old clothes were taken away and burnt, and we were given trousers and a shirt and old Indian shoes. We found ourselves all looking rather disreputable and like beggars, but at first we were quite cheerful. We made tea and sang and danced in the evening and the Indian officials encouraged us and cheered us up. But áfter a few days rest we began to wonder what next? The Lama and Doté Chandzo were taken very soon to a special centre for Lamas at Buxa near the foot of some hills further to the west. The rest of us stayed in the camp.

We organized ourselves into groups of ten or so, and drew our rations through one of the group and cooked them ourselves. The food was not bad, but it was now May and very hot. After a few days we began to feel the heat and to be worried by the dust, the flies and the mosquitoes. It was impossible to sleep at night, and we felt weak and breathless. The cheerfulness of the first few days soon wore off and the Indian officials became busier and busier and more and more worried. We had been among the earliest arrivals and the camp had been fairly empty, but as more refugees continued to stream in every day the strain on the Indians got worse. They had little time to talk to us or encourage us any longer.

The Camp Commandant was a brisk, short-tempered, Indian officer who got very angry if things were not done exactly as he said.

There were other Indians to help him and some Tibetan interpreters and junior officials who acted as our spokesmen. It must have been difficult for them to know what to do with the growing number of refugees. When new arrivals came in, the Lamas and senior monks were usually taken to Dalhousie or Buxa. Some of the laymen were taken away, too, probably to work on roads; but to those of us who were not sent off anywhere, it seemed that the choice was haphazard; perhaps the Indian officers did not realize at first that we Dob-dob would work just as readily as the laymen.

That really was the worst part of it all, having nothing to do. I often went with my friends to the Camp Commandant and asked to be sent somewhere where we could find work. We also volunteered for any job that was going in and around the camp. I was lucky to be taken on to carry wood and water for the Indian supply shops and, I got Rs 2/ a day which was a great help. Most people by now had little or no money left and had sold almost everything of value they had managed to bring, usually for a very poor price.

Before long the rains began. Everything was soon deep in mud, and the mould, smells and corruption worried us. The water, too, was terrible. We could hardly bear to drink it and many people fell ill. Everyone suffered from sweating and prickly heat and it was particularly hard on the old and the weak. Some mothers had walked all that weary way from Tibet with babies or young children, and because of the effort and exhaustion they had no milk and the babies died. There was a lot of fever and stomach trouble and all sorts of illness. It was heartbreaking to see the suffering in the camp and the hospital. There were not enough doctors, or bedding or medicines and some of us used to go to help in the hospital by taking food and water to the patients.

One day, Pandit Nehru came to visit the camp. We all gathered round and he spoke to us through an interpreter. He called us his brothers and said he was very sorry for us and that we should all try to work. We clapped very hard when he said that because work was just what we wanted. Some of the refugees performed dances and sang for him and his party. One thing that surprised us was to see ladies, both Indian and European, being given better seats and placed higher than some men, even higher than Lamas and monks. Women are treated with respect in Tibet but that is a matter for the home and, in public, they would never take such a position.

My best friend in the camp was Sonam, whose room I had shared long ago in Sera and who had been with our party on the journey from Lhasa. Some other *Dob - dob* of Sera also joined our group and we did what we could to pass the time, going about to look for work, or playing games or chatting. There was no privacy for anyone; but the learned monks who were kept in the camp made great efforts to pray and meditate or study. Most of us fixed up a sort of low bed to keep us off the wet ground, and some monks managed to make a flimsy partition round theirs, in an attempt to get a quiet place.They would sit there with their backs to the central gangway of the hut, facing the wall, reading books or concentrating on their meditation exercises hour after hour, in spite of the heat and flies.

Sometimes we visited the bazaar outside the camp and although we had very little money the Indians there were sympathetic and did what they could to help. At first the people had screwed up their noses and made faces and said that we smelt, but they soon became friendly and spoke kindly to us. We used to give them any rations we could not eat, and they were pleased with that.

Time dragged on like this. Those of us who were left behind felt envious and unhappy when they saw parties, including many people who had arrived long after us, being sent off to other camps. We thought anywhere must be better than Misamari.

After some months a real disaster struck me. I had a sort of warning in a dream, in which two friends and I were walking outside the camp and saw an Indian carrying a load of wood on his shoulder. One of my friends said "Don't touch the wood"; but I did touch it and it burst into flames and I was all burnt up. It was a very bad omen but I did not tell anyone about it. Three days later the blow fell.

Some of us had gone one day to cut down a dead tree outside the camp for firewood. Another man was hacking at the trunk and I was standing by when it fell. I was not really very near but a branch broke off and part of it hit me on the leg. I was knocked over and felt a sharp pain in my leg and when I looked at it I saw the bone sticking out near the ankle. My friends carried me to the hospital and eventually a doctor put on a splint. But the leg did not get any better. It was agonisingly painful and began to go bad. My friends took me to the Camp Commandant and asked if I might be sent to the American hospital at Tezpur, quite near the camp; but he said I should stay in the camp hospital. My leg was bandaged again and I just had to stay where I was but as the pain was terrible my friends became very angry and kept insisting that I should go to the American hospital.

I became very sad and depressed and wondered what would become of me. The pain got so bad that although Sonam did everything possible to help me, I often thought of killing myself and was looking about for a way to do it.

Eventually, the camp doctor decided that I must have my leg cut off and that I should go to the American Mission hospital for the operation. Although my friends were relieved that I could go there at last, it was terrible news for me. I wept bitterly and wondered how I should ever be able to live and work with only one leg.

I was taken to the hospital in a jeep and the American doctor there was very kind and distressed because I was so miserable. I refused at first to let him cut off my leg and he was even more worried and told me that if I did not have it off, I might only live another five days at the most. I said "I don't want to live, let me die". But Sonam kept encouraging me and said "You have two arms and will have one leg left. Don't be a fool. You will manage all right. We will look after you". So I had the operation and my right leg was cut off well above the knee. Perhaps if I had been able to go to the American hospital sooner I would have only lost my foot. It was a terrible feeling when I came to after the operation and found I had only one leg.

I was kept in the American hospital for about a month, and was very well looked after there. The Indian nurses were kind and there was an American lady doctor who came to see me as well as the doctor who had cut off my leg. Sonam was allowed to stay with me at first and he and another *Dob-dob* friend called Chukchi gave a lot of their blood for transfusions for me. I would not be alive but for them.

Then I had to back to the camp. That was pretty bad. I got there at night and I could not get my own things which I had left in the care of the Camp Commandant, but I was treated very kindly by the people in the camp. All my old friends except Sonam had gone, but some recent arrivals took me into their hut and gave me tea and food. I was very weak still and found it difficult to get about with only one leg and a stick.

Next day I went to get my things from the Camp Commandant

and begged him to let me go to Dalhousie where the rest of our party had been sent; but he said I must stay. And then another terrible thing happened. Sonam was sent off to Dalhousie. We went again to the Commandant to ask him to send me too; but again I was refused.

Now I was almost in despair. My best friend had gone and more and more people were being sent away every few days so that the camp was becoming empty. The new friends I had made were sent off too, and at one time I was all alone in a great empty barrack hut. People helped me so far as they could. The Indian and Tibetan workers in the rations store saw that I got food; and they made me bedding out of some empty ration sacks. Other people brought me water and I tore down and burnt parts of the empty bamboo hut for fuel. I went to an English lady, Mrs Bedi, who was helping the refugees, and I asked if she could do anything for me. She gave me a good shirt but could do nothing to get me sent to Dalhousie.

Then one day a Khampa whom I had never met before came into my hut and said he wanted to help me. He was a wonderfully generous person. He went and got work so that he could buy meat for me, because I was so weak still that I needed better food than we got in the camp. He looked after me with great kindness and brought some of his friends to help me too. Of course, he was taken away to some other camp before long; but he left two little Khampa monks called Tenzing and Gompo to look after me. They were quite young but were both very clever, and were bookmen monks who could read well. They managed to get work with one of the camp officials and brought the money to me. They were so kind and cheerful that I began to feel happy again. They looked after our shabby hut as though it were a monk's cell. It was always clean. They made a little garden outside, planted five banana trees for shade, and went to the river and cut turf to make a raised bank to sit on. It all looked so pleasant that our hut became very popular, and many people came to sit and talk with us. We had a little alter inside at which the boys regularly recited prayers.

Gradually I got stronger and was better able to look after myself and get about more easily. I began to hope again that I would be able to go to Dalhousie. Then, at last, I was told that I was being allowed to leave the camp. But it was not to go to Dalhousie. I was to be sent to Dharamsala because that is where arrangements had been made to look after old and feeble refugees. Still, that was better than staying at

Misamari and I knew that the Dalai Lama and some of his officials were at Dharamsala so there was hope of getting more help there.

I was told that I would have to go on my own with a party of old people but I made a great fuss and insisted that I could not get on at all in that way and that the old people would not be able to give me the help on the long journey that I still needed. So I begged that Tenzing and Gompo should be sent with me. To the joy of all three of us, that was allowed.

A party of more than a hundred of us, old men, women and children, were taken by lorry to a railway station and put into a train. It was crowded and hot and the journey took a very long time; but we got enough food and we did not mind all the trouble and difficulty because we hoped we were going to a better life. I certainly could not have managed without the two boys. It was not easy getting in and out of the train when we stopped and we wanted to go for water or to relieve ourselves. They were very careful of me and tried to prevent people from crushing my leg, which was still painful. But it was quite a job sometimes when I had to be pushed in through a window of the carriage.

After about five days we arrived at Pathankot, where we left the train and were taken to a camp with a lot of Tibetans in it. From there we went almost at once in lorries to Dharamsala. It was wonderful to go up from the hot plains into cooler country and lots of trees again. In Dharamsala we stayed in a house in which we had a small room, like a monk's cell, and were given food and clothes.

I soon discovered that Shasur Theiji, who had been kind and friendly to me in Lhasa because he was the uncle of the late Sharpa Lama, was living in Dharamsala, where he was now a Minister attending the Dalai Lama. I went to see him and he was very sympathetic and helpful. He often sent his steward to me with presents of food and money, and he made arrangements for me to go with other refugees and receive the Dalai Lama's blessing. His Holiness noticed that I had only one leg and asked me very kindly about it and told me how sorry he was.

The best help of all that Shasur gave me was to have me sent to Dalhousie to join my old friends. It took a month or so to make the arrangements and in the meantime I was quite happy at Dharamsala. The two boys got work cleaning peoples' houses and they earned good money, which they shared most generously with me. They learnt to speak Hindi very quickly. I did what I could to help some of the old people who were being looked after at Dharamsala.

When the time came for me to go to Dalhousie it was decided that the two boys would stay in Dharamsala. We were all very sad. They had been always so cheerful and so good to me and we had become very close friends. But Shasur advised us that they would have a better chance of education and of finding useful work if they stayed, and he arranged for them to be taken on to help in a nursery home for little children, which was being run by the eldest sister of the Dalai Lama.

It was still winter when I left for Dalhousie. I was taken there in a bus with some old people who were being transferred to a new camp for them there. It was after dark and snowing when we arrived, and as I was not going to stay with the old people I did not know where to go. I just made myself a shelter in the snow by the side of the road with my baggage and slept there. The next day I was able to find someone who knew where Sonam was staying and who took a message to him. He and several others of my friends soon came to welcome me and take me home and we were all very happy.

Dalhousie is a lovely place, with plenty of trees and lots of good water. We lived there in a good wooden house that held about forty people. But they were all out in the daytime, working or going to the training school, so I was alone quite a lot. I was much stronger now and I was able to look after the house and to do most of the cooking. Sonam was earning Rs 2/ a day and he brought meat, milk and eggs for me to help out the rations that the Indian government gave us. There really was little to complain about, and I was getting used to having only one leg, though now and then I forgot about it and when I tried to stand up normally, I fell down. It was not easy to get about in Dalhousie because it is a hilly place but I managed with a stick, although it was rather tiring. Of course I wanted to do what other people were doing, and at the New Year I went out with Sonam to get wood. We climbed up a fairly steep hill in the snow and that was really too much for me and made me very tired and quite ill. My friends looked after me very well, but it is an uncomfortable feeling to be different from everyone else.

I discovered a strange thing, that some people seem to think there is something unlucky about a man who has had a misfortune. One day I saw coming in my direction a young monk I had known quite well in Sera who had belonged to the same Khamtsen. When he caught sight of me he turned aside and walked up the hill to avoid meeting me. I felt deeply hurt, and began to think again how useless and hopeless I was. I began to weep and be miserable. But there were not many people like that, and one monk whom I hardly knew at all came up to me one day and said how sorry he was for me and pressed some money into my hand.

My special friends were always trying to cheer me up. We really had quite a comfortable house, with enough to eat, and time to play games. And when the weather grew warmer we went out to bathe in the streams and took our food with us for a picnic. That was all pleasant enough but it did not occupy my time, so when I looked about for other things to do I found that some of the refugees in another house were starting a dance group to perform the Ache Lhamo dances. I was able to help them by making masks for the dancers. I had learnt this in Lhasa and it was not difficult to make the triangular masks worn by the Hunter actors in the dances. They should have been made of leather and decorated with cowries, but cardboard did quite well and white buttons and the like took the place of the shells. Also, I knew the flute music and most of the steps of a peacock dance, which I had learnt from one of the famous companies of dancers and actors who came to Lhasa every year. I made a basket frame for the figure of the peacock and covered it with cloth, and we managed to get a lot of feathers from Pathankot. Between us we taught some boys the dance, and it was performed when Indian or foreign visitors came to visit the camp.

Even so I had not enough to do and began to get bored. So I asked the Camp Commandant to let me attend the school where our refugees were being taught boot-making, weaving, paper-making and so on. He was a very kind officer who spoke Tibetan well -- he came from Bashahr I think -- and he took a lot of trouble to find work for us. The school was some way from our house and was up a steep hill, and it was quite hard work climbing up there so I did not go back to the house with the others for the midday meal. They taught me to weave and I spent a lot of time weaving carpets there.

None of us could guess how long we would have to go on like

this. We all wanted to go back to Tibet as soon as possible, but whenever any new arrival managed to get away from the country we heard bad and depressing news, that the Chinese were taking over all the villages, punishing and imprisoning anyone who had any land and taking away their property. Very few monks remained in the monasteries; most had been made to leave and either put into prison camps and made to work on roads and drains, or had been persuaded to marry and become farmers. It seemed that most of the people who used to live in Lhasa had been sent to other places, but no one really knew what was happening.

XVI
"GENLA" AND PASANG

There seemed no reason why that sort of existence should not go on forever. Then, one day after I had been at Dalhousie for about eighteen months there happened the next unexpected change in my life.

I had a strange feeling of excitement in the morning and wanted to go to the training school much earlier than usual, but Sonam said I would just have to wait. So we went at the usual time. About midday a foreign visitor came to the school with a Sherpa friend. I saw them going round the place looking at everything and asking questions. The idea came to me that I must talk to them but I did not dare to say anything.

After the visitors had gone and I had had my lunch I still felt restless and excited and I decided to go down to our house. I was hobbling down the hill on my stick when, as I had almost expected, I met the two visitors. They couldn't help noticing me, but I was surprised when the foreigner spoke to me in Tibetan and very kindly asked what had happened to me. So I was able to tell him all about it with the help of the Sherpa who was called Pasang, and I asked if they could help me to get an artificial leg.

The foreigner was Dr. Snellgrove, whom I call Genla, and the Sherpa Pasang had been on several journeys with him in Nepal and had gone to England with him too. When they spoke to me I suddenly felt that here was someone who could help me. I began to hope again. Genla found out where I was staying, and promised to let me know what he could do.

That evening he sent a message that I was to go to the hospital in Dalhousie. Next day he was there too, and saw that I had the stump of my leg examined and measured so that an artificial leg might be made. He took me to his hotel and gave me tea and food and some money, and told me not to expect too much, but that he would let me know what to do next. Then he and Pasang left Dalhousie.

I waited about three weeks and then a letter came telling me to arrange a helper and to go to Pathankot to meet Genla. One of the Tibetan officials arranged a jeep for me, but I did not know what to do about an interpreter so I went off alone. At Patankot I found that Genla was visiting Dharamsala but he had sent two more Tibetan friends of his, Sonam and Lopon Namdak, to meet me. I discovered that they were probably going to be taken to England by Genla to help him in studying Tibetan books. Sonam was a young lay official of a noble family in Lhasa who had escaped from Tibet soon after the Dalai Lama and had been in Misamari camp, but only for a short time, so I had not met him there. Lopon Namdak was a very learned Bonpo Lama who escaped through Nepal where Genla had met him.

The next day Genla arrived himself and we all went off by train to Delhi. It was a very different journey from my first. This time I was travelling in comfort like an official. I was quite respectably dressed in a fairly good Tibetan cloak for, as Dalhousie was quite cold ,most of us had managed to get some sort of Tibetan dress. But I had to learn quite a lot about how to live and behave with foreigners. Pasang knew all about it and was very good at teaching the rest of us, and we all got on very well together and were cheerful and happy. I could hardly believe what was happening to me.

In Delhi we went to stay at an ashram belonging to some monks from Ceylon. It was very clean and pleasant and the first thing that happened was that Pasang and Sonam gave me a good bath. Genla gave me some light weight trousers and shirts and very soon he took me to the hospital. That, too, was quite different from the other hospitals I had been in. The plan was that I was to have another operation to tidy up the stump of my leg, then be fitted with an artificial leg. Genla himself was going back to Nepal with the others, so he left money for me and arranged with a Tibetan official, who was in charge of our refugees in Delhi, to fetch me from hospital when it was time to leave and look after me until Genla got back from Nepal, where he expected to be for about two months.

So I was by myself again but I did not worry too much. Although there were no other Tibetans in the hospital, I could get on by now in a sort of Hindi and the other patients were friendly. The doctor and nurses looked after me very well. The operation was quite small, and then I just had to wait for the new leg. When it arrived I found it rather heavy and clumsy, being made of wood and leather. It felt very strange at first but I got used to it, and it was a great improvement on having only a stick. That all took two or three weeks and then I was ready to leave hospital. But my troubles were not over yet. The doctor sent word to the Tibetan official, but days went by and nothing happened. No one came to fetch me, even though the doctor sent more messages. Fortunately, the doctor allowed me to stay in the hospital. If he had not, I would have had now here to go. I was anxious of course, but not seriously worried, because I was sure Genla would eventually find me again. He had even said that he might think of taking me to England when he went back, and, although I could hardly believe that, I thought he would certainly want to see the new leg he had arranged for me.

In the meantime, as I was really quite well and much better able to get about I could make myself useful to the other patients and help those who couldn't leave their beds. They were always calling for water or the bed pan and I was glad to help them because it kept me busy and I was sorry for them. It was a help to the nurses too. In fact, as I was now feeling very cheerful, I became quite a favourite and they all liked trying to talk to me. On two occasions, two Americans came to the hospital to look for me. I think they must have been friends of Genla but I never discovered their names. They gave me sweets and fruit, and I am sorry I don't know their names so that I can say thank you.

As time went on and I had no news of Genla I decided I must try to do something. I got the doctor to telephone to the Tibetan official and I spoke to him myself. He said he had forgotten about me. I was very angry and perhaps rather rude, because I knew the doctor had sent messages to him and telephoned three times at least; and I knew Genla had left money to pay for my expenses. I told him that, and asked him to send for me at once. So his son came and took me to a rest house where he was staying, and where I got a room and meals for which Genla had paid. The official paid little attention to me, but I helped in his garden and did odd jobs to keep myself occupied.

After a week or so the official said that perhaps I ought to go to Kalimpong because there were a lot of Tibetans there. I did not want to go there because I thought Genla might never find me, so I said that if I had to go anywhere I would go back to Dalhousie. Fortunately, just as

I was getting really anxious, Genla appeared. He had not been able to find out where I was and had come to the rest house only by chance. In fact, he thought I must be in Dalhousie and had bought a ticket to send me so that I could come back. I was very happy to see him again and he was quite surprised and very angry that his arrangements had been spoiled by the Tibetan official. He was rather annoyed with me too because I had had my head shaved. However he took me to a restaurant where I had my first taste of ice cream but I didn't think much of it and I have never come to like it much.

It appeared that Pasang was in Darjeeling with Sonam and Lopon Namdak and two more Tibetans whom Genla had decided to take to England. They were Sangye Tenzin and Samten Karmay, both Bonpo Lamas. Genla said we would go there and join them and we would travel by aeroplane. That was exciting as I had never been in an aeroplane before. It was quite a short journey and very comfortable and we could see all of Bengal beneath us. I had my first beer on the aeroplane and I did not like it much, but that is a taste I have quite easily acquired. In Darjeeling we stayed with a friend of Pasang. There were many Tibetans there and I was happy to meet my old friend Dawa, who had been in Kyirong and was now a trader and doing quite well.

One day Genla took me for a walk and asked me all about myself and whether I would really like to go to England and help to look after the house where the other Tibetans would stay. He said, too, that he was not pleased with my new leg which was too heavy and clumsy and that it would be possible to get a better one in England. I said that I was quite ready to go. Then he asked me about the various names by which I had been known and said he was going to call me Tashi. And so, although some of my former Tibetan friends still call me Lhakpa, I have been Tashi to most people ever since, and that is a good name because it means good luck.

Genla was busy making arrangements to take us all to England. There were a lot of papers and permits to be got as well as places in an aeroplane to London. Genla had to go to Delhi and other places, but it was decied that Lopon Namdak and I should wait in Calcutta, and that Pasang should take us there by train. There was a bit of trouble on the way because when we came to Siliguri, where the train started, the police tried to stop us going on. We had not yet got the right sort of passports. We argued with them and tried to explain, but they would not listen. At last I said "all right, take us to prison". However, Pasang, who had proper papers, was able to get in touch with Genla, who came and put things right. I thought how clever and important he was to be able to make all these arrangements.

It was very hot in Calcutta, where we were to spend ten days before leaving for England. Genla had arranged with some of his friends to let us live in a flat in their house. We were very comfortable and had our own kitchen, where I learnt how to cook on gas. Our hosts lent us a car and driver and we went all round Calcutta and did our own shopping. I remember that we drank a great deal of Coca Cola, because that was the only drink we knew how to ask for. We were both much puzzled at first by the wife of our host. She was young and slim and had quite short hair and wore trousers. We thought she was a boy and were surprised to see her husband kiss her when he went out or came back home. A great many things seemed strange to us about living in a foreign house, but our hosts made everything as easy as possible although we could not speak a word of each other's language.

From Calcutta we were to go by air, through Delhi and Rome, where we were to meet Genla and the others again. We had been sent our papers and tickets and Genla had also fitted us out with good Tibetan clothes. Lopon Namdak had a fine new set of monk's robes and I wore a Tibetan cloak, which had been well made in Delhi, good trousers and a white shirt. With my artificial leg that sort of dress was more suitable than monk's clothes.

Genla's friends saw us off at Calcutta. We travelled by Japanese Air Lines and were surprised how big and comfortable the plane was. Meals were served by pretty Japanese girls, and although we could not talk to them Lopon Namdak who was a vegetarian had learnt to say "I don't eat meat". When hot towels were handed to us we didn't know what to do with them; but we watched other people. The only real difficulty was when we were given forms to fill in before reaching Rome. We had not the faintest idea what was wanted, but a nun who was sitting near us came to our help with all sorts of signs and gestures with her hands, and she filled in something or other into the forms.

We reached Rome early in the morning, and were rather worried because there was no one to meet us. However, Pasang arrived after some time and before long the whole party -- Genla, Pasang, Sangye, Samten, Lopon Namdak and I — left in another plane for London. We arrived there in the evening and went to Berkhamsted, where Genla had a house in which we were all to stay until another house could be found for us. His neighbours, who later became my very good friends, had prepared dinner for us. And that was the beginning of my life in England.

XVII
LIFE IN ENGLAND

We had expected London to be hot, like India, and were pleased that it was cool and fresh -- it was September when we arrived. The last week or so had been rather rushed and bewildering but now we could settle down and look around. There was a great deal to learn and Genla and Pasang must have had lots of problems at first. Genla gave us lessons in English and Pasang took us out shopping and explained what we saw going on all round, and how we should behave. We all helped to look after the house and garden and most of us learned to cook. Genla is very clever at that, and took great trouble to teach us. Although I was a good cook of Tibetan food it took time to learn new ways, and I remember some of the pastry I made at first being almost too hard to break. I remember, too, being scolded for rubbing butter on my face as we used to do in Tibet.

Genla took me to Roehampton, where I was measured for a new leg. Very soon I had one, far better and lighter than the one made in India. I had to go back now and then for the doctor and fitters to see how I was getting on. They were the kindest of people and took a great interest in me. Of course, even with the best artificial leg the other one has a lot of work to do and I get tired fairly quickly, but I really get about very well.

Sometimes we went to London and visited the important places, but I did not take in much at first. The whole place was so crowded. Everyone was in a great hurry, and the smell of the traffic was awful. All of us felt quite sick because of it and Lopon Namdak, in particular, was miserable. I suppose one gets used to it, but I still notice it in the streets and am happy to get away to places where there are no motors. And we found the crowds confusing. They simply streamed past without looking at anyone else. There were crowds and busy traffic in India too, but there people notice one another and it does not seem so much like living in a machine. Because we were accustomed to being surrounded by people with dark hair and small noses, we noticed the large number of people with fair or red hair, bright red faces and big noses.

After about six months Genla managed to find a flat for us in a house near Primrose Hill, in a quiet street with fine trees and gardens. It was quite new and Genla furnished it nicely and we lived there very comfortably except that as it was on the third floor it was tiring if I had to go up and down stairs too often. I stayed in the flat and looked after it most days while the others went to work at the University of London. I went there too sometimes, to English classes. Many guests and visitors came to the flat, and they always seemed to enjoy the meals we made for them. Sometimes it was Tibetan food, but usually it was simple, well-cooked meat and vegetables done in the French way, and salad, cheese, wine and coffee. Genla was particular that everything should be done well and I came to like that sort of cooking very much, but as for drinks, I prefer beer to wine.

When we had settled down and learnt some English, Genla took us for many tours by car in England, Wales, and Scotland. We all enjoyed getting out into the country and especially the mountains. Genla took me with him to Europe, too, and we travelled in many interesting and lovely places in France, Switzerland, Italy and Denmark. There are so many wonderful cities, palaces, cathedrals and churches to see. We were often reminded of Tibet but some of the churches in Europe are very plain and, although a great many have beautiful paintings over the altar and fine gilded decorations, I don't think any have such splendid golden images and ornaments and jewels as we had in our chapels and cathedrals. I like seeing lights burning on the altars, but am always rather surprised that they are put out when a service is over; we think they should be kept alight always. The music and singing were very impressive and most of all I like the chanting, which is quite like that in our monastery assemblies.

Best of all were the monasteries. We visited a great many; and sometimes were allowed to stay in Quarr Abbey in the Isle of Wight. Life there was like Tibet in many ways. It was quiet and plain, and everyone was devoted to religion. We noticed that in Europe all monks work with their hands, not only lay brothers but even the most learned, while in Tibet the bookmen monks would not work in the fields. I think it is good that all monks should work with their hands, though those who are learned should spend less time on that than those who are not so clever.

As well as church music, I came to like other foreign music from hearing it on the wireless. Genla has a good gramophone and lots of records which he played to us. Because I play wind instruments, I prefer that sort of music and, although I often like the sound of a big orchestra, there is usually too much going on at the same time for orchestral music to be followed easily.

After some years our household gradually became smaller. Pasang went to France to learn how to make wine, and he is now back in Nepal in charge of a new vineyard. Sonam went back to India and is teaching in a Tibetan school. Then Sangye and Lopon Namdak also went to India, and only Samten and I were left in England. The flat was now too big for us and I went to stay with Genla in Berkhamsted, while Samten got a room in a University hostel. Then Genla bought two old cottages in Tring and had them converted into two small houses. One, with three bedrooms, a good sitting room and a large library room, became Tibet House where Tibetan visitors could come and stay and work with foreign scholars interested in Tibetan matters. Many of Genla's friends gave a great deal of help in building the house, fitting cupboards and in making a little garden with a paved court and small pool in it.

I was given the job of looking after the house, and had a nice room to myself with a small altar and plenty of space for my clothes and books. Quite a lot of the time I was alone, but I like being by myself for a time. Genla was not far away in Berkhamsted and I knew all my neighbours and the people in the shops. In fact, I found Tring a much pleasanter place than Berkhamsted, and — because it is smaller -- people are more friendly. I used to go to a pub nearby where everyone called me "Charlie" and made me welcome.

There is fine open country near Tring and I used to go to the Chiltern Hills to fly kites. Tibetan kites are very simply made and can be turned out quickly -- just a matter of thin split bamboo and paper, nothing elaborate like some of the kites I saw other people flying. But ours are far more efficient and kite-flying was a great sport in Tibet. We used to have tremendous fights when we dressed the string of the kite with powdered glass and tried to cut the other man's kite free and perhaps capture it. I think we are more expert in kite-flying than most people here, and when I fly mine watchers are often surprised at the height they can reach in a very short time, and the way they can be made to dive almost to the ground and then soar up again.

There are big reservoirs, too, near Tring, and one of them is a splendid place for swimming. Genla very wisely encouraged me to learn to swim, because with only one leg it is tiring to take much exercise in almost any other way. I never tried to swim properly in Tibet and not many Tibetans can. In fact, quite a lot them get drowned when they go to bathe in the rivers, or take horses to wash there. I was taught by an instructor at the University swimming baths and used to go at least once a week. Now I am a strong swimmer and enjoy it very much.

Probably the most valuable thing I have learnt is how to drive a car. A good friend, David Johnston, taught me. I had to have hand controls fitted but even so I did not find it easy and it took a long time. Often I almost gave up hope; but David was very patient and eventually I mastered it and am completely at home in a motor so long as it has the right sort of controls. I have driven in many parts of Europe as well as all over Britain, and have never had any real trouble. It has made me much more independent and useful.

There are quite a lot of Tibetans in Britain, including a party of children at the Pestalozzi school at Sedlescombe, perhaps about forty of us in all. And representatives of the Dalai Lama sometimes come to London, so I meet my fellow countrymen here from time to time. I found many Tibetans in Europe, too, on our tours there. In France and Italy they are mostly scholars, but in Denmark and Norway they learnt various skills and most of them have gone back to India to help their fellow refugees. In Switzerland there are a great many Tibetans earning their living in all sorts of ways, working in cheese factories, bakeries, timber yards and on farms. I suppose they will stay there permanently. Once, when Sangyé and I were travelling together by train in Switzerland, we sat opposite four young men who looked rather like some Eskimo we had recently seen in Denmark. Eventually we heard them talking Tibetan so we spoke to them. They had thought we might be Chinese. We were all amused because we thought we would be able to recognize fellow Tibetans anywhere. It just shows what a different hair cut and different clothes can do.

Now that I have been so many years in England I feel entirely at home. In fact, not long ago I became a British national. I think I must be the first Tibetan to have done that. But there are some things we Tibetans do not get used to easily. It is still quite a shock to see people walking in the street with their arms round each other's necks and kissing one another; and the couples who lie about making love very openly in the parks seemed quite shameful to us at first. Tibetans do not pretend that sex does not exist; they can enjoy it and make jokes about it, but to behave like that in public is regarded as very bad manners and immodest. It took a little time, too, to get used to the rather casual way in which people meet and talk, which is done with much less formality than in Tibet. And it seems to us that children are mostly less well-behaved in Europe than in Tibet. They often appear to be bad-tempered, and quarrel with one another, and are allowed to make a great deal of noise; and they do not always do what their parents tell them. If it were possible, I would be quite happy to go back to the quiet easy-going life in Tibet. As it is, I should not be much use with one leg and I could not get the treatment I get now when I need it. But I am sure I could get on somehow and could easily do without such things as gas and electricity, and even a motor car. Perhaps what I should miss most, of the things I have become used to here, would be having plenty of hot water for a bath whenever one wants it.

I was able to see how many of the Tibetan refugees in India and Nepal are getting on, and the kind of life I might have been living, when Genla took me there in 1967. That was an exciting journey, all the way in a Land Rover. I was only a passenger because the car did not have hand controls. We visited some wonderful monasteries in Greece, perched on the top of mountains like Tibetan hermitages. Some of them could only be reached by being pulled up in a basket. And we saw the huge statues of the Buddha at Bamian. Near there our Land Rover was almost washed away in a flood and we lost some of our clothes and things; but we got to India all right.

I met some old friends there, and I saw how a lot of the refugees are settling down in farming communities. Others have formed their own groups and are making carpets and boots, or silverware. Yet others were earning a living in companies performing Tibetan drama. There are also settlements of monks and several new monasteries and chapels but, of course, they are much smaller than in Tibet. A great many children are attending schools and doing very well; only those whose parents are working on road-making in mountain country on the northern borders are not so well looked after.

My oldest and best friend Sonam was doing quite well, making boots at Dharamsala. It was a great pleasure to see him again and to be able to help him a little, as he had done so much for me. I could not meet the two boys who had been so kind to me in Misamari, as they had been sent to Simla to work on the roads. I was sad to learn that Shasur Teji had died not long before; and I could not find anyone who had news of Tshapanang and my family. Doté Chandzo was in Buxa but had gone out of his mind. The governor of Kyirong was somewhere in India and I heard that he was teaching in a school. I did not make any effort to see him.

Genla took me to receive the Dalai Lama's blessing. It was a very simple ceremony and nothing like the receptions in Tibet. There His Holiness sat on a high throne in a hall of the Potala or Norbu Lingka, surounded by the monk officials of his court and household, with the highest lay officials sitting in respectful rows on one side of the hall and more monks on the other. We monks from Sera were formed up outside the hall into a closely packed line and were kept strictly, sometimes quite roughly, in order by the Dalai Lama's bodyguard of specially tall powerful monks who kept shouting "close up! close up!" When we entered the hall each of us prostrated himself with his head to the floor, three times, then we took our place in the line again and when we reached the throne, pulled out a white scarf from the front of our robe and handed it to the Chamberlain standing beside the throne. Then we stepped up a little and passed in front of the throne, our heads just coming up to the level of the Dalai Lama's knees as he sat there cross-legged. He blessed each of us with a touch of his hand as we passed, and a monk official on the other side dropped a small strip of knotted red silk on our shoulder. We tied the little scarf round our necks as a mark that we had received the blessing.

But at Dharamsala His Holiness received Genla and our small party by ourselves. He was standing quite simply in front of a chair in a western style room and there was only one assistant with him. He spoke freely and kindly to me and asked how I liked England. He told me not to forget to do all I could to help other Tibetans. It was wonderful to be so close and to hear him speaking like that.

A lot of the Tibetans we saw in India and Nepal were living in quite poor conditions, but they mostly seemed cheerful and ready to work. Generally, they were helpful to one another. I thought that the Indians in some villages I saw were almost worse off. Certainly we never had such poverty in Tibet as I saw in India.

In Nepal I met a nice girl from East Tibet and thought I might marry her and bring her to England, but so far I have not been able to arrange it. I should say that after so long a time away from Tibet I find it hard to go on being a monk. It is really impossible to lead that life unless one is part of a monastery; and as I was never educated I cannot read and study the religious books. So, not long ago, I gave up my vows to the religious teacher at Sedlescombe. All the same, I can't help feeling almost a monk still, and I often think of what we were taught about behaving properly to all our fellow creatures.

Tibet House in Tring had to be closed in 1969 and, as Genla's work took him to Italy for much of the year, I had to find something else to do. For a time I looked after a fine hall where concerts and plays were performed now and then. It belongs to a lady living in a beautiful old house, near York, surrounded by lovely parkland and fields. I enjoyed the quiet country but although I had good friendly neighbours it was rather lonely. Later I was lucky to find a new home with very kind friends who treat me as one of the family, and where I hope I am useful too. Looking back on the past 12 years, I see that my karma has led me in an unexpected direction from the Tibetan village where I was born. I have been cut off completely from my own family life and the life of the monastery and from most of my old friends. And I have lost a leg. But I realize that I have had a surprizing amount of kindness and good fortune; so perhaps the name that Genla gave me -- Tashi, Good Fortune -- is really quite a good one.